I0039250

# PEOPLE
# Power

## What Happened To People Of African Ancestry

## Dr. Sadiki Che' Baye

| | |
|---|---|
| Type of Work: | Text |
| Title: | People Power: What Happened to People of African Ancestry |
| Copyright Claimant: | Dr. Sadiki Che' Baye, 1951 - |
| Date of Creation: | 2015 |
| Published: | 2016 |
| ISBN: | 978-0-692-03170-4 |

Library of Congress Control Number: 2015960649

Copyright © 2016 by Dr. Sadiki Che' Baye.

All rights are reserved by the author/copyright claimant. No part of this publication may be reproduced, stored in a retrieval system or transmitted in any form or by any means electronic, mechanical or otherwise without the prior written permission of the author.

Printed in the United States of America

# Contents

## Dedications

## Pearls of Life

# DEDICATIONS

This book is dedicated to all the people of African Ancestry in these Americas; to my spiritual teacher, mentor and friend: The Honorable Dr. Haile Baba Olugbaba Amen-Ra; also to my beautiful, loving and hard working mother, Queen Mother Henrietta Samuels Willis, both who have passed on to be Ancestors. Happy New Life!

I give thanks to all of the Elders and Ancestors who inspired and motivated me to continue to give and make a positive impact on others by being the example.

A special thanks to Sister Abanaa Carter for typing my manuscript. I also want to express my appreciation to Mrs. Florence R. Givens, who is a self-published author of many books for taking the time to read and critique my manuscript; her advice has been invaluable.

# "PEARLS OF LIFE"

These are my "Pearls of Life" given by our Creator and inspired by our ancestors and elders. These are pearls of universal knowledge and inspiration to all who embrace them. Be Wise!!!

1) Keep your mental and spiritual lights on at all times. Make sure that they are always bright. There is truly a way to always keep your Mental and Spiritual Lights on. Never put an "on or off" light switch, always put on a dimmer switch, which you can turn the lights up, or you can turn the lights down, but it is always on. Guess What? Some people are so obvious with their nonsense that you do not need a light, but keep them on anyway because they can create illusions, especially if you care. The more you care about someone, the harder it is to let go! So, we eventually give them a free pass to do and say what they want. If you are true to yourself, then you have to go Old School and not

pretend that it is not going on. If your lights (Mental and Spiritual) are on then, that should cause you to see what is before you. Never ignore the sign, no matter who or what it is. It is what it is! Never ignore a person's reality, especially your own. The Truth Is The Light! Turn all your lights on Warriors! The time is now. Tomorrow is no guarantee. Just because you were put, or forced, or fooled, or manipulated, or lied to, you do not have to stay there. Every man must find his way. Keep your Mental and Spiritual Lights on at all times so that you can see without pretending or faking. Be Real! "To Thine Own Self Be True!"

2) Always remember to stay strong and keep your faith where it belongs: faith in your Creator and your people. Everyone must understand the Need to learn about the Laws Of Life, in order to know how to read signs of Life. No one is exempt when it comes to testing and trying your strength and your faith. How would you know the true you if you were not given an opportunity to prove yourself worthy of who and what you are for Real? Always remember that

all of us will be challenged. Welcome the challenge, but first, you must recognize what it is, no matter how painful, hurting or discomfort the situation may be. Nothing outside of you should be greater than you if you are God-centered. That is the goal! We must continue to Transform and Renew our minds. That means you have to continue to lose your life to gain your life. Everything and everybody must change because nothing remains the same! Remember That? How well we can sing that, but do we really believe it? Your choices will define you. If you are growing and learning, you can't go wrong because you will find that life is all about the process. Most people are afraid of processes, especially if it pertains to them personally. Why? Because through the processes, they will have to truly face themselves. It can be ugly and scary. That is why we should always be Honest with ourselves first and take a regular inspection of the Man In The Mirror. We need to man up and woman up for our future-The Children. Also, put a smile on the faces of our Elders, while they are here. Put an intentional smile on their faces because they earned it and they deserve it. Don't forget that your turn is coming. My people, Always Stay Strong And Keep Your Faith Where It Belongs. We can do it! We are the original. What is better than original, but original!

3) Do your best and let God do the rest. In other words, you should know when to hold and know when to fold. We must always put forth our best efforts, no matter what the situation and circumstances are. You are the greatest creation of all times. That's right because we are the Original Man (Mind, Thinker) that can do all things if only we believe. According to your personal beliefs, it will manifest in your life where everyone can see the results. As within, so without, Cause and Effect, you can fool some of the people some time, but some people you can not fool at all. The Elders and Ancestors did not always say anything; they would just look at you and shake their heads. That meant that they were aware of something about you that you thought that you could hide. Old School

people were very Wise and Clear-Mind-
ed when it came to understanding Life's
Principles. That is why they always said
to live by principles because God is always watching. We must Honor those
before us by embracing the "Blueprint
of Life" process that they were blessed to
have and leave to follow by the ones who
are here and the ones to come. By ignor-
ing that can cause deep and long lasting
problems that most people are struggling
with today. We must better our best in
order to transform into our godhood nature, which is the ultimate goal of Man.
"Be ye in the world but not of it." Always
remember that we have to give Our Creator a reason to be there for us. We have
lost our sense of direction, by design.
"Seek and ye shall find." and "Knock and
the door will be open." Now we must ask
our individual selves, do I really believe
that? Most don't, but everyone is held
accountable for his own journey and
choices. No one can fool or manipulate
God-Life! If you are true to yourself you
will always do your best when it comes
to your own personal growth and de-

velopment. Righteous people are hated with no just cause. Be aware so that you can keep your Balance. The bottom line is for us individually to do our best always. Then we qualify ourselves for God to do the rest. In other words, leave it in His hands. Some people feel that God is not moving fast enough or that He don't know what He is doing. So, they take it back what they gave Him. That is one of the worst things that one can do in life when you don't trust and believe in Our Creator. He said that He is a jealous God and there will be no others before Him. Beware of the worldly things because they can give you a false sense of security. Don't act like you do not know! We are all blessed through our efforts. So be blessed! Our Creator want to help us but we must qualify ourselves by doing our best for ourselves and each other. The bottom line is when you have done all you can with the matter, then leave it in the hands of Our Creator-God. Prayer causes things to change in your favor if you are sincere. He knows our hearts and so does His people-The Remnants. Let go and let God!!!

4)   Last but not least, keep your head towards the universe where all strength comes from, and never give up, and never give in, no matter how things seem. Everything is, always was and always will be in divine order. Keep The Connection!!! We as a people are the Original People of The Most High! Remember that He made us in His image and likeness. That means that He did not make any mistakes when He created us. We got to know that we are all that, but someone's planted weeds in our garden while we were sleeping. That tells me that we need to wake up and not allow the weed-planters (wicked) to plant without our permission. Take your God-given position and plant a beautiful weedless garden. Keep a watchful eye on your garden because weeds can grow unexpectedly. Everything needs maintenance. But timing is very necessary. Always know that once you get there, you have to maintain your position which will be challenged. Know that you are a child of God! Our main purpose is to rise above this world and claim our right-

ful position as part of the Universe. Our Creator gave us dominion over all that He created, even you. Any man or woman who is willing to challenge everybody, whether they are right or wrong, and not challenge themselves have to be in the category of being a Coward. That's right! When you are afraid of yourself, then you have a lot of diseases going on within. How can you be about healing yourself when you are scared about what you see in the mirror? Our Creator said to fear no one but Him. I guess when you are out of order, then nothing gets done. Always keep your Mind's Eye towards the Universe where all strength comes from. We must no longer keep our heads down buried in the sand. We must lift our heads toward the Universe where our Power comes from. Be the Universal Man that we were created to be. We are not a star in the universe, but a star as the universe! Remember that my brothers and sisters! I am because we are and because we are, I am. When you keep your head toward the universe, then there is no doubting. Muhammad

Ali was a great example of no doubting. He believed that he was the greatest, and he was. No one can say I am for another because it is personal. Always believe in yourself and your connection with the Universal Movement.

(Law of Karma) of the conditions of the African-American people who have lived and died in the "United States of America." We as a people have suffered in many ways for no just cause, other than to profit off of us, which is still apparent today. Too many of us are in denial based on the fears that are within. When one does not challenge their own self, then how can you move forward unless someone is carrying you. We must no longer rely on our own misunderstanding of self and the ones before us, who were living in hell. We must show an appreciation for the ones that paved the way and gave us a blueprint, an opportunity to become great once again. We must be students of life principles once again. Sankofa!

"There is very little that is more important than for any people to know their history, culture, tradition and language, for without such knowledge, one stands naked and defenseless before the world." (Cicero)

Indigenous people of the continent of Africa, formerly called Alkebulan, "The land of the gods" or "the land of the spiritual people," were despised ever since the Europeans (Caucasians) and Asians (Arabs) set eyes on them. Jealousy and envy of the Africans by others developed into hatred with no just cause other than wanting to be like us, and have what we have or had.

# PREFACE

As a result of these unjustified racist attitudes, the Africans were forced into slavery. Most of the slaves were brought to America to build a superior society for a barbaric and savage people – the Europeans. Africans throughout the world are known, without a doubt, to be the "teachers of civilization." (Chancellor Williams)

Now that America is second to none, thanks to the people of African ancestry, the Euro-Americans are creating ways of genocide because they feel that they are finished using Africans to build this empire. As a result of slavery, people of African ancestry in America have been almost totally stripped of their history, language, and culture: their total identity. This created a new people with no identity, who are trying to be something that they are not, or have no idea what to become; no direction, and no purpose. Subsequently, they have become a confused people! Check out their conditions physically, mentally and spiritually. Be true to thyself, make it real and keep it real. You may be hated for that. But, in spite of that you have to and must fulfill your purpose unto God, Our Father. The One God!!

As Malcolm X stated, "just because kittens are born in the oven, does not make them biscuits."

This applies to Africans born in America. Just because one is born in a different geographic location, does not change his or her nationality. Since Africans in America were enslaved and treated in such a vicious manner, they have been identifying with their slave-master, the Euro-American enemy. The present day people of Africa in America, off-spring of the indigenous Africans, who have been degraded and dehumanized, have been hypnotized to be everything except for who they really are - the original man from the continent of Africa. Please make yourself aware of your-story (our story). Seek and ye shall find. Knock and the doors will be opened. Never give up or give in! Only the truth will set us free. If the truth is the light, and we are living in darkness (a Lie), then the light will cause us to see. Since we are living a lie, we are going through life, generation after generation, in a haphazard manner, bumping into obstacles and falling blindly into traps. As a result, we willfully forget, willfully avoid, willfully ignore, willfully pretend, and willfully disrespect one another. America is set up to guarantee failure for Africans. All one has to do is look at our overall results: suffering out of want or lack of wisdom and understanding. "To Thine Own-Self Be True."

African-Americans must be about the business of knowing their history and culture by studying. Only when this happens, with understanding, will they become free and independent. Freedom is not given, it is earned. We must organize, plan, strategize, and work it by any means necessary.

Our individual purpose is to make it better for yourself and transmit it to the group. In other words, make it better for your people.

Today, we must be made aware that we are the architects of our life. We can build for ourselves a virtual paradise when we begin to know who we really are by nature – godly: the original people who taught the world civilization. Know Thyself. For if you know who you really are, then you will know who God is. Never Forget! Always Remember!

If we would make our world right, we must first right ourselves individually. Our first duty is to ourselves. The first law of nature is self-preservation. Each individual has an obligation and responsibility to prepare themselves for the group (team people) for the advancement of their purpose, which is to live forever using our ancestors as a frame of reference. Sankofa! Sankofa means to go back and get what is necessary to create positive progress.

In other words, never forget your past because you might have to go back to reinforce where you are. Life is about balance. It should be our duty to inform ourselves, to invest our life with righteous generating practices, and to live so that we'll not only experience life for the great joy that it can be but become a radiating example of the highest human virtues, as our ancient ancestors. We must follow the blueprint which was given to them by our Creator. Study to show yourself approved. A real man (mind) will come to his own conclusions. Think first!

Since there is a cause for every effect (The Law of Karma), we must be made to realize the erroneous concepts and practices in America, beget errant results. Equally, we must be made to realize that only if life is led in harmony with nature and truth will we appreciate the highest rewards. Right thinking, right eating, and right giving develops great people (Refer to the Alkebulan Magazine).

When looking at the conditions in America, it is plunging headlong into self-destruction through suicidal pursuits and practices, which is headed by racism. Racism is defined as the notion that one's own ethnic stock is superior (Webster's II New College Dictionary). This debasement and perversion of human behavior must be reversed, especially by the African-Americans who were and most are still hypnotized into a stupor. Real people are not popular people because their mental lights (wisdom and understanding) are always shining. Everyone, turn your lights on! Stop living in the dark (willful ignorance).

It is the duty of us who know the truth, to do what we can to contribute towards waking up our people mentally first! Our duty, as aware individuals, is to first put our house in order. We must become a model or example, devote our resources and energies to prudently and wisely bringing righteousness to the attention of our brothers and sisters. We are gregarious people by nature. We need each other as never before. Each person must step up to the plate and hit a home run for the team. We must develop into team players. The group is the key: unity, community (common unity).

"Be ye in the world, but not of it" (King James Bible). In other words, how can you rise above the world? The only way that you can do that is you have to be about the process of bringing out the Godhood in you, and then assist (encourage) others to do the same. Before you can become a team player, it is vital that you find and foremost get your individual self together. You have to prepare yourself to become a team player according to the purpose! Don't forget that the team is only as strong as the weakest one. We all have to become team players! It took a team (father and mother) to get you here, and it is going to take a team to sustain you. Don't be fooled by individualism, which means that it is all about me. The devil turned the "M" in "Me" upside from "We!" Understanding is the principle thing to strive for! Either you are growing, or you are going!

"Choose you this day," says the Lord (King James Bible). Your choice! Everyone has a free will! We must strive to become the Gods that we are. If everyone says that they are a child of God, then that means you are like your Father. That is why our Father said that you are made in my image and likeness! But, everyone has to find their way! Religion is just a way you choose to get to your spiritual self. Whichever way you choose, make sure that it is causing you to seek your spiritual self: your Godhood! Since man means 'mind', 'a thinker', then we must be the way that our Father intended for us to be.

Let's get down with the process: Right Thinking; Right Giving and; Right Eating!!! We must become whole! Someone has devised a strategy to fragment us and has done a masterful job to accomplish that. Take a holistic look at us. Look at the effects from the causes! The things that were forced on us was, and is so diabolical that it is a wonder and a miracle that some of us can think! There are very few thinkers, but we are the remnants that our Father said will always exist! We are group oriented by nature, and we must become natural again. "Let's get back to the original way of life." Everyone has something within to offer. You are blessed through your efforts. How much effort you expend will determine your blessings! Beware of that always! We must fight hard and smart from within to overcome our confusion that was and is given to us. If a snake is a snake, then why do we have a tendency to forget about that? Beware of the nature of a snake, and then you can understand why they do what they do. We need to be the eagles that we are, because eagles eat snakes as a meal, like breakfast food. We must fly or rise above this world and start looking in!!! You have to really want it!"

# Chapter I

# Culture

Culture is a highly developmental state of civilization, tradition, and customs. It is known and generally agreed that mankind originated in Africa. That means that Africans are the fathers and mothers of mankind. Many people will hate you for telling the truth, but it must be told and never forgotten.

History is an accumulation of thoughts and past events which have been pasted on orally; by inspiration; or by written narrative. The entire past of humanity sets forth the constructive achievements of man as abilities, traces the rise and growth, and sometimes the decline of civilization or culture.

Civilization derived from Latin *civilis*, "pertaining to a citizen" referred to the social condition existing under the forms and governments of the classical city-states of a people. Historians interested in man everywhere and at all times, often prefer to use the unequivocal term "culture" or "groups of people" rather than a term which carries with it the implications of a rigid distinction between low or primitive peoples and high or advanced peoples.

The fairest types of humanity, the highest achievements of the human spirit are found among people whose physical life is considerably advanced in the practical arts and sciences. The indigenous people of the continent of Africa, the Mother Culture and Civilization of the world, originated mathematics and all the arts and science of civilization. Humanity, in order to maintain a peaceful solution among various class interests, has in the course of its history resorted to many forms of governments and religious beliefs. Arts and sciences are what give our people a sense of identity. It causes us to always use our divine minds and ways to create monuments and all forms of imagination and creativity that all can bear witness. Such as, pyramids and many other symbols and structures that originate with people of African descent.

Many Blacks had lived in America before we were brought here as slaves, while some were forced to come. We must understand that we populated the world before Europe was there. Do your homework on Queen Europa and you will be shocked to know that the continent was named after her, whose roots are from Africa. Always keep in mind that I give Food For Thought. Our existence is noticed all over the world and the universe. Study to show yourself approved, but you have to come out of your comfort zone-The Box.

# Dr. Sadiki Che' Baye

When you are in the box, everywhere you go there is a dead end. Most people are afraid of coming out because, in order to do that, there can be a lot of pain, hurt, and discomfort that most people are not willing to challenge. We must find a way to Man Up and Woman Up!!! We need to reinstate the Rights of Passage, which means each individual have to prove themselves worthy of joining the Team. In other words, becoming a Team Player. It should always be about the Team. Get yourself together for the Team. Cooperation and preparation are the main ingredients for unity-One Aim. Anyone can do anything that they put their minds to. Never make excuses when it comes to qualifying yourself for the upliftment of the Team.

From the earliest times, men who have knowledge of supernatural powers or gods have exercised political power in order to maintain peace and order in societies, no matter the class. The roles played by our traditional priests support this assertion. Priests were heads of the state religion which he was occupied with a constant round of sacrifices, ceremonies, prayers and festivals on which the welfare of his people depended on daily. In religious matters, the king was assisted by the priests. They grew ever more powerful as the kings lavished treasures of gold, silver, paintings, and etc. on the temples and endowed the priestly corporations with landed estates exempt from taxation which is still practiced today.

# *People Power*

Take a conscious look at the major churches, temples, synagogues, and mosques of today. The so-called rulers (government and corporations) have no regard or respect for spiritual leaders.

The king's relations with them were not always friendly. For instance, during the reign of Ramses III, a ruler of the Twentieth Dynasty, was overthrown by the chief priest of Amen at Thebes, who himself ascended the throne. Most religious so-called leaders today are very passive, misleading, and cowardly.

They must start telling the truth and nothing but the truth. First and foremost they have to be willing to go over and beyond their programming. Most of these so-called learning institutions can take you further out left field. We must acknowledge that, especially when you are striving to be an excellent student. That can result in being an educated fool. After that, you will pass on the lie and confusion. The truth is never in the box which creates nothing but illusions and a false sense of, "I am well educated." Education should be defined by those who you came from, the ones who look like you and have the Creator that looks like you. That is right ladies and gentlemen. If it is not in your image and likeness, then you must start asking questions that are Necessary. Turn your mental lights on my Brothers and Sisters for your own awareness, so that you can see what is before you and what is behind you lurking in the dark (wickedness and confusion).

They go along with the government to also control the masses for their minds, money, women and children. The ancient name of Egypt is Khment or Kemet, which means Black Land and the Black people of the Nile Valley, is the specific geographically area that I am referring to.

Culture is the center of one's history. When men live together and work together, they create culture together. Men have always formed themselves into groups, clans, or tribes and by design, someone was usually appointed as head, king, or chief to direct the affairs of the group in any way. This was necessary in order to enable the community to perform its traditional functions of maintaining law and order, defense and protection from external attack on any member. Whatever men build or do to preserve culture must be done by them as individuals, for the group.

Everything a man does is according to his conscious level. Growth and development are determined by your level of understanding of self first. Therefore, the group concept is the key to continuation. It is the love of oneself and the group that will result in a desire or tendency to seek to promote that, which is in their own best interest of direction.

Every vision, implement, mechanical device, or machine is nothing but the materialistic manifestation of an idea, which preceded it in some human mind.

All beliefs, customs, traditions, and institutions whether simple or complex, must likewise originate in the ideas of individual minds. Nowhere else can ideas originate. Man is mind! This is a physical environment of inorganic matter, climate and a social environment of fellow men. Each molds the individual man, groups and by promoting or retarding the growth of ideas helps to determine the growth of the culture. Environment is the key. Man depends on nature. He discovers, appropriates, and transforms natural energies, but he does not create them. Adaptation is necessary, or he will perish. To live is the primary and fundamental human activity.

Today, man's mind is so absorbed in what he sees, that he doubts the vast realities that he does not see physically and mentally. The present makes him blind to the past and the future. He is fooled by glory, and illusions therefore fears not a fall.

Take a good hard look at our behavior today that promotes the destruction of one's circumstances and eventually their lives. What A Waste! All of this can be avoided if we take another look at what is happening to us every day, especially our youth and our Elders. We have developed an attitude of, "I don't give a damn." Some people can not help themselves because we must remember that, the harvest is plentiful, but the laborers are few. Also, many are called, but few are chosen. Don't be too surprised or shocked to see and know that some of them are ones who we care for. That is when you have to be careful and know when to hold and know when to fold. Easy said than done when you really care about the individuals. But, you must find a way to not allow them to interfere with your divine Purpose.

Our first obligation is to our Creator, and each other. That can only happen when you have a spirit of unity, which is based on total cooperation and willingness. Do all that is necessary for the Team To Win! Absorbed in disaster, he gives up hope and sometimes faith. Man must study nature and history, and restore his faith. No one can appreciate themselves and where they are until they know where they came from. The open minded person will come to his own conclusion. Righteous Judgment!

Culture passes from generation to generation which assures the existence. Bad social practices, natural calamities or warfare can destroy a culture.

Immaterial culture is handed over and handed down, to others in part by spontaneous imitation. Children imitate their parents; we all imitate one another. Transmission of immaterial culture also takes place by means of perception, training, and discipline, in short, by education practices. Any cultural feature not preserved in one of these ways must be discovered or invented anew. Otherwise it ceases to exist. Those who fail to take heed to the blueprint that has been passed down through our

Ancestors will no doubt be killed or destroyed by their own creation that is not in line with their culture. Always study and remember what was before us before the disaster. Go Sankofa! Seek and ye shall find. Know that your faith will always be tested and tried. Do not be discouraged.

These are prime examples of what is happening to African-Americans. In order to prevent the disappearance of their culture, they must quickly return to the centerpiece, which is their families guided by God's principles! People of African ancestry, all over the world, must teach their children that they are direct descendants of the greatest and proudest race who ever peopled the earth. It is because of the fear of our return to power, in a civilization of our own, that may outshine others, is why we are hated and kept down by a jealous and racist world. We need to remember our own past and do something that reflects a free people, a free spirit. A God People!

I understand today that we have been taught to do our own thing, which resulted in being individualistic. The average female of today will tell you easily that she does not need a man. What a damn shame because we can not do without each other. How do you think all of us got here. It was the efforts of a man and a woman. That is Family! A lot of this individualism started growing out of hand when we so-called integrated. We integrated with people who taught their children to do their own thinking. In other words, to be independent of the group. The system taught us that the individual can be more important and better than the group, when in fact, we are group oriented people by nature. When we so-called integrated, we gave up too much of our own cultural ways. For instance, we closed or shut down our businesses and supported theirs as though theirs was better and more righteous. I don't know, but that sounds like we volunteered to take ourselves right back to slavery, because of a false sense of feeling that you are better. We've been lied to again because freedom is not given, freedom is Taken. Any Means Necessary! Every group of people must find their way independent of all other groups. That is how you get Respect. The people of African descent were fooled to believe that integration will make us equal finally. How can you be equal to someone who have 400-500 years start on you? When we start minding our own business, we can zoom pass all others quickly, and they know that. That is why they work so hard to keep us down and out of our minds. If we were really stupid, then why do they continue creating ways to keep us in that condition? When in fact, stupid people will always keep themselves down. No one respects stupid people because they don't even respect themselves. Since we were taught to be something that we are not, it causes us to do any and everything that is against us. Life have no tolerance for ignorance and emotions! We, as a people have been hypnotized to believe that, "oh well that's just life."

That means that we have assimilated to the lies and deceptions that the world has given us. Let us all wake up before it is too late, because our children and Elders must be saved and protected (spiritually, mentally and physically) to have a wonderful life that we have intended for them to have and cherish. We must fight hard and smart to change our circumstances, which is a result of our choices. Change your choices, and we will see positive results that will benefit us forever. If not, we will get the same results multiplied.

For instance, acquiring all kinds of diseases and suffering as the enemy is getting. Isn't that what is happening today? We as people are getting diseases (not at ease) that were everybody's, but ours. But when you live the lifestyle of a diseased people then you will get the same. Remember, the environment dictates all! As a people, most of the diseases we never heard of until we integrated, and now we are cursed by them because we refuse to mind our business as the Original People. We must cooperate with Life's Principles or suffer the way all other people are doing. We can do it because we were created to do anything we put our minds to do. Step It Up Warriors for your own divine existence!

The transmissive process depends fundamentally on the use of verbal language, whereby man communicates to his people those general ideas which make up his culture. Since African-Americans have adopted someone else's language, and lost theirs, they are on the verge of losing their own culture. To re-establish their culture requires the usage of the language of their Ancient African Ancestors. They must get back to their roots: Africa. They must first find out what their strengths and weaknesses are, and then work towards bringing forth whatever is beneficial for the whole. Man has a responsibility to give back what he has been blessed with (physically, mentally, and spiritually). We must reflect our Father God, just as the female must reflect her man.

Discovery and invention are dependent on the physical environment, which may or may not furnish opportunities, to advance a culture that is looked upon as improvements, provided as necessary stimuli. The larger the social group and the denser the population, the more numerous are the needs which must be satisfied by the ones who are involved. Urban living causes a major problem with people of African ancestry. We as a people fight extremely hard to keep the illusions of our conditions going so well that we are "equal in rights" like all the others, but we will never make that happen until we show (action) some respect for one another.

Love without respect (the foundation of all relationships) is definitely Not Real! The roots of the tree of knowledge sink deep into the culture. African-Americans should take heed to prevent the total disappearance of their culture. Get back to the land: Nature! Nature has no tolerance for uselessness and/or ignorance. That which is useless is without purpose or substance. Negativity cancels itself out! Life is about peace, harmony, balance and truth. Let's get back to the original way of life.

Diffusion generally implies a voluntary borrowing of culture elements, but this occurs only when the new elements can be fitted into the group life, thought and behavior. European culture was forced on Africans for over four hundred years. Africans were forced into slavery and made to deny their culture, language, history, tradition, and religion by the so-called civilized Europeans.

Missionary activity illustrates the diffusion of elements of culture by conscious, forceful training and instruction. European religion was carried throughout the world by missionaries who have aimed, not only to convert other peoples but to introduce among them their own moral and social standards of living and thinking. Advertising, organized propaganda, physical force, intentional mis-education and motion picture must be included among the racist who have become responsible for the diffusion of culture for African-Americans.

Culture elements are more often derived from one group from another than independently discovered or invented, for the simple reason that it is usually easier to imitate than to originate. This is a perfect condition that has occurred with today's Africans born in America. Nothing is more familiar than the fact that an entire people may use the same speech, accept the same beliefs, obey the same laws, attend the same schools, observe the same customs, follow the same fashion, and in short, possess many elements of culture in common.

There is a uniform group culture, which may be compared with that of another group. Africans in America and all over the world need to take an extensive examination of themselves to determine their plight. Man should be one culturally, as he is one spiritually, mentally and physically. We are an under-developed people because of our lack of understanding of our Ancient Ancestors culture. Freedom implies responsibility and accountability. We all have to be responsible and accountable for what happens to ourselves, as well as our communities and what takes place in them on a daily basis. Education of one's self is the first law of nature. Know thyself, for if you know who you are, then you will know who God is!!! "To Thine Own Self Be True."

Nevertheless, men differ with respect to logical power, imagination, creativity and capacity for abstract thought; and their environments differ. It is not surprising, therefore that African-Americans should have cultural diversity. Differences of culture exist within the same group: witness the familiar contrasts between town and country, north and south, east and west, or between social class. These differences become accentuated between groups so that every society possesses a certain degree of culture uniqueness (spiritually, mentally and physically) enabling it to make a special contribution to the life of man. African people, you have a culture of your own! "Seek and ye shall find..." Life is a journey. Be honest and true to yourself. Call everything for what it is. It Is Always What It Is!!! When, and if you cannot measure it, it does not exist!

All institutions are cultural products and are established to maintain and advance a cultural way of life for all who participate. For instance, schools exist for the culture. Culture comes before the schools. If there is an existing culture already established and people from another culture participates, don't expect the existing culture to provide you with your needs unless you are participating to add to your own culture. The pitfall for Africans living in America is that they expect the Euro-Americans to provide them with an African cultural way of life. America has its own cultural way of life and Africa has its own cultural way of life, and neither should expect the other to provide them with another's culture. The purpose of participating in someone else's cultural ways should be to add to your own cultural ways, to advance.

Institutions reflect the culture and change as a result

of cultural change, such as schools, religion, food industry, government, occupation, and etc. to insure the existence. It is the cultural desire to maintain and to go beyond itself thru understanding that creates the need for institutions; consequently, achievement motivation and self-determination must exist in the culture before there are institutions, which serve principally by which certain achievement motives attain their own ends. Hence, institutions, including performance and commitment in them, reflect their cultural roots. This is why the black "uneducated" ghetto parents understanding little of the requirements necessary for American academic success, can be of little or no help to her child in acquiring the necessary skills to make such success possible. American culture does not reflect African culture because they are two different uniformed cultures. The lack of an educational tradition and unity in the ghetto home adversely affects the parent's ambitions and vision for the careers of her children. One must know one's own culture before participating in someone else's culture, or you will be imitating someone of a foreign nature, which is happening today. Institutions for chickens cannot teach an Eagle how to be an Eagle!

Even though they are both birds. We must understand that they are two different kinds of birds. Why are we as an African-American people the only ones that believe that all people are the same? Know and understand that we are different people with Godlike skills. Everyone knows that there are different kinds of every species. That is the beauty of our Creator to create different kinds of everything! We are Unique people because we are the Original, which means that we are the First. But someone's brainwashed us to believe that all people are the same. Don't go for the super lies that have been forced on us for so long that we actually believe the lies. Rise up my people and Take your Rightful place in life. Our Father is waiting for us!!!

No one can be about the business of change unless they change their way of thinking. It is actually thought that changes people, "As a man thinketh, so is he." We must build and sustain each other. We must develop our courage to overcome what is wrong on the inside (mentally and spiritually). If we stand where we are, then we can do it together! Beware of individualism! Unity is key! Oneness!

## NOTES

## NOTES

## Chapter II

# Man Power

Energy is discovered, appropriated, and transformed by man. He is a pensioner on nature. With plants and animals, the adaption to the physical environment is chiefly direct, involving modifications and adjustments of the body structure; with man the adaptation is chiefly indirect, producing cultural change. Man's association-al life, gradually accumulated and then transmitted to new members of the group is what produces culture. Everything of culture is the center of one's history. People who live together and think together grow to have a certain resemblance. For instance, the people who are African descendants who live in America have become more American than the Euro-Americans. It can be safely said that it is a result of four hundred years of slavery: dehumanization and degradation. The majority of African-Americans have become like zombies (living dead) who are people that are always about survival, just making it, accepting little or nothing, hopeless, very emotional, left out, detached, no vision, depressed, oppressed, pressed, and so on. Violence has become the solution to everything. Fear is the driving force. Respect must be restored as the foundation! Respect yourself first and then you will have some respect to give. You have to have it to give it.

Too many people have become the great pretenders. For example, when two or more come together, you will find someone who is carrying a hidden and selfish agenda. First, they will establish themselves as a child of God. They say, "I believe in God more than anything, He is my rock." Remember those phony people? Their game is to get everything for themselves, but claiming they want a respectful and loving relationship with you because "I like your style." Their scheme is to only like what they want and what they can get and will always want theirs, when in fact they have very little, if any, to give or offer. Good people always give his people the benefit of the doubt which is almost always taken as an opportunity to get what they viciously want. Beware of the "good looking snake" because they are deadly. It does not matter what you call the snake, always remember that a snake is and will be a snake in the grass!

Giving the benefit of the doubt is what we owe each other since all of us have been bitten one way or another. Healing comes through each other! We got in this mess together, and we must come out of it together. Respect for one another is the main ingredient and foundation to all real and lasting relationships. As a child, we were taught to respect everybody no matter what. Today we teach our children to love everybody with no foundation which is Respect. You have to have it to give it! People say that even a dog deserves respect when we forgot to give it first to ourself and then we will have some to give to one another.

When you are out of order, then you will see the results of it. You can run, but you can not hide, especially when it is what it is. Disrespecting each other should have no place in our lives toward each other. All of us been had, but some of us are more Healed than others because of our efforts. Everybody is blessed through their personal efforts. Some people put the cart before the horse by saying that, "I love you." When in fact, they don't even respect me. That is out of order, and there will be some serious consequences that you can not prepare for.

Everybody played the fool one time or another. Learn from it and be Wise! Today is all about love with no solid foundation, and that is why for the average person love comes and goes. Everything that exists has a foundation, and the stronger the foundation, the more you can build on it, and it will last. The man is the foundation of his relationships because he is the head. He must always show and execute the characteristics of who and what a man needs to be.

Sounds like we need to go back and embrace the Rights of Passage, from an Ancestral point of reference; being 21 years of age is not good enough. In other words, action speaks louder than words. Today, words speak louder than action. Most people feel that they don't have to prove anything that they say. Execution of what one says is proof that they mean what they say. When you see things today, the ones who show themselves approved are hated and despised. The scripture says that the good people are hated with no just cause. Don't be deceived by the haters, especially those that you care for, the ones who have those fantastic titles because they can hurt you more because you sincerely care for them, and they know that. Most people use your kindness as a weakness. Set yourself free with the truth no matter how much it hurts. Always remember the first Law of Nature, which is Self-Preservation. Everything that is real is relative; connected and enhancing.

Historically, we have a race of people going into another people's country (Africa), kidnapping them, along with killing them, and taking them to a foreign land and made to be slaves for them. This was viciously and insanely done by Europeans (Caucasians) to the indigenous Africans. Not only did they kidnap the Africans, but they brought them to a foreign land which they stole from the indigenous Indians. Blacks who were already here.

The so-called Indians were no one but the same people who originated in Africa. We are brothers and sisters that happen to be on this land together to do the Will of Our Father, forever. The land is what is called today, America. The land of the so-called free. The Europeans even used the Bible as a justification to enslave Africans. They stated that God gave them the right to conquer the world by using Blacks to achieve their mission.

Propaganda, which brainwashed most people, spread information throughout the world that Black Africans were uncivilized heathens. With this in mind, if it were true, then why would a so-called civilized people kidnap an uncivilized heathenish people to build a superior society for them? Would a president of any business or corporation use unskilled people to start the foundation of his structure? Of course not! If he plans to succeed, he will use intelligently skilled personnel. Being that America today is second to none, the foundation could not be less than superior. Blacks in America, who are the descendants from Africa, are no doubt the foundation of the country of America.

Europeans created a master plan to rob the Indians and all Blacks who were already here on this land that is called America, of their land (America), and uses the Africans to build their society. Their aim was to use the superior skills of the Africans to build a superior society, for Europeans; that will make life good and easy for them. Today, we must understand that power is global, and control is local. We take our situation for granted. We blame each other for our problems when in fact, we are manipulated by the system (American controllers) which are forces that are against us. Ignorance of one's self is definitely deadly and suicidal. "The First Law of Nature is Self-Preservation."

If you read and study history, you find that the Africans who were kidnapped were Kings, Queens, scientists, doctors, lawyers, mathematicians, agriculturists, and etc.. This does not sound like uncivilized people at all. When you want to control a people, first you have to study their lifestyle and behavior. The Europeans found out about the godly nature of the Africans, then they created a scheme against them: posing as their friends. The Greeks, who were the first to study in Africa: Herodotus, Socrates, Plato, Aristotle, to name a few, stated that the Africans were truly "gods" of the universe. These Greeks studied under the indigenous Africans and were called the "fathers" of philosophy and medicine. They forgot to say the fathers for the Europeans. The great genius and African, Imhotep, was the original father of medicine and science, who was worshiped as a god for three thousand years. Hotep means Peace! During this time the Europeans (Caucasians) were very heathen, barbaric and truly uncivilized.

Was envy the thing that caused the so-called civilized

Europeans to enslave the so-called uncivilized Africans; who are today the Black people in America? A real man will come to his own conclusion based on concrete evidence. Fair Judgment! Wake up and see the truth.

Slavery was a nightmare to the Africans. Their entire history, culture, religion, language and tradition was taken from them. How? If you look at American history, you find that the Euro-Americans beat and maimed Africans into submission. Hundreds of thousands and even millions of them were even killed. Families were viciously separated and sold to different plantations. That left the innocent children, at the mercy of the white master, which ended up to be our great-grandparents. Our great-grandparents, descendants of Africa, were made to denounce who they were and where they came from, and to accept the white man's ways, which were inhumane and against nature and God. How can a people do such vicious acts and call themselves believers? If they are believers, then one need to look into who and what they truly believe. You definitely will be shocked! Check it out for yourself. (See Reference: "Destruction of Black Civilization by Chancellor Williams).

## The Body

The diet habits of the men who first appeared on earth were said to be vegetarian, as recorded in Genesis 1:29: "And God said, Behold, I have given you every herb bearing seed, which is upon the face of all the earth, and every tree, in the which is the fruit of a tree yielding seed; to you it shall be for meat." Historically speaking, Moses was the writer or author of the book of Genesis, which was not the beginning of man; but of a religion. Going farther back into history, one finds that man was even a breatharian, which means to live on pure air. There is recorded history that in the beginning, man was first breatharian; liquidarian; fruitarian; vegetarian; flesh-eater; and today a "garbage disposal." These stages of man's diet indicate a numerous amount of falls. There are today some breatharians that live in the highlands of the eastern world that live on pure air. This to some people is unbelievable, because of the state of the modern day popular diet: flesh-eaters and "garbage disposal"; people eating anything.

Approaching life without knowing and practicing your own culture, is like traveling through life without Light-Vision (wisdom, knowledge, and understanding). Most people die of Want or Lack of Wisdom! When you disregard Life's Principles, you must and will suffer the consequences! Look at the major state of mind in America. It is very destructive. All crisis is a danger and an opportunity to grow in every way. Beware that everyone will not react the same way. Some will be creative, and most do not want to be creative. That is a God given right: Choices!!! Be careful with your choices, because they create results accordingly. Most are Rebelliously Stupid, Willfully!!!

Since the vegetarian (vegan) diet is the most popular of all, let's consider this the most natural of the modern diets. The vegetarian diet compared to a meat-eating diet is more healthy. If one goes back to Ancient Africa, where man originated, you will find that man did not kill for food. The Africans were in harmony with nature and did not have to kill for anything because the forest provided them with food and shelter. The body was given the food which it is made to consume. Man has soft, pliable, cup-like hands with flat nails that ideally suit him to gathering food from the trees.

He also has 32 teeth; 16 in each jaw; four incisors; two cuspids; four bicuspids; and six molars. The cuspids are adapted for cracking nuts, and the articulation of the teeth enables man to mash and grind nuts. A natural diet of fruits, grains, nuts, seeds, and vegetables are the only requirements for our great machine. It is no wonder, then that countless studies have proven that vegetarians all over the world are far healthier than those who eat meat.

Cancer is practically unknown among the vegetable-eating natives of Central Africa, although these people became addicted to flesh eating by contact with whites, either on the African coast, in America or Europe. They soon began to show great susceptibility to the disease. The disease has increased tremendously in all civilized countries. Dr. Senn, after an extensive study of the diseases prevalent among the natives of the east of Africa, report that he found no cancer and no appendicitis among the non-flesh eating tribes of this part of Africa.

Gautier calls attention to the fact that oxalic acid and other poisonous acids are among the products of the oxidation of flesh foods in the body. "On a flesh diet these toxic bodies accumulate and acidify the blood, excite the heart, and intoxicate the subject, disturbing the functions of the skin, lungs, liver and kidneys."

All food comes originally from the vegetable kingdom, and it is better to take it first-hand than second-hand. The function of food is to supply the energy needed to support the work done and to keep the body in repair. Forty percent of the energy used in digesting the meat is wasted and also alike percent of energy used in the elimination of the urea and other waste products derived from the meat. Meat not only produces and aggravates gastric acidity through its direct stimulating effect upon the stomach but also encourages intestinal putrefaction and constipation, which caused gastric acidity. Flesh which is unusable material causes unnecessary taxation of the liver and kidneys, which contributes to their premature failure and the development of disease in these important organs. In the U.S.A., 95% of the population have heart disease, approximately 80% are overweight, have cancer, poor or no elimination, artherioclonosis, harden blood vessels, and on and on.

It should not be forgotten that meats of all sorts contain a considerable amount of toxins, which are the result of protein putrefaction (rotten). This is always true since meat, as eaten, is in a state of beginning decomposition and consists in part of the poisonous waste substances which are always found in animal tissues and which accumulate rapidly after death. It is well known to sanitarians that animals often suffer from diseases, which are directly communicable to human beings through the eating of their flesh. For example, trichina and tapeworm, two horrible parasites, are never acquired in any other way than in the eating of flesh. Tapeworm is usually derived from beef, and trichina almost universally from eating pork. Of animals eaten by human beings, the hog, the barnyard fowl and fish are the only ones, which include flesh in their bill of fare.

Meat is made tender by the process of putrefaction and is always kept to "ripen", a process which involves putrefactive changes due to the presence in the meat of the terrible bacillus, the cause of gas gangrene; a common putrefactive organism, so-called "prime beef" and "high" meats are sufficiently advanced to please the palate of a vulture or a buzzard. This is aged meat after death. Many people are losing their passion for life by making poor choices. The main cause could be because they don't know who they are or who they need to be, and most are not even interested. Therefore, they suffer and blame everyone and everything but themselves. Learn the Law of Karma. Everything is Just and Nothing Just Happens!!! Keep on Learning and Adjusting, no matter how things seem. You are The Greatest!

Meat eating is a popular notion which is based not upon scientific observation or experiments, but upon preconceived opinions and prevalent customs. At the present time, these false ideas are being actively fostered and propagated for the promotion of the financial interests of the livestock and packing industries. In the United States alone, nearly 9 million creatures of God are slaughtered daily for our supposed dietary needs. Those of you who weep if and when your dog or cat were killed, go on silently condoning the needless slaughter of millions of animals each day.

We kill animals in cold blood, in other words, take the lives of innocent beings, then we bury their carcasses in the pits of our stomachs, as do the savage beasts of the forest. Some of us raise the animals and then kill them and bury them in our stomachs. That is vicious and inhumane: The American Way of Life. Instead of treating the illness, we need to treat and heal the person. Until then, will you feel a need to adjust towards being healthy? When you are in Control of Yourself and Your

Behavior, you don't have to think about control because you are in control! Practice is definitely Necessary! Be Patient With Yourself!! Allow Time To Heal Through Your Efforts!!!

Lower animals are adhering more closely to the divine order in diet than is civilized man with all his intelligence and knowledge. The degeneration of man has threatened to destroy the whole human race, and will ultimately accomplish this unless the present rapid, downward trend is checked and reversed by a return to the natural or biological life. We have to learn how to appreciate what is true! Order of Yourself is First, Know Thyself!!! There are more people who do not care than people who do care for real. Life is for the Living! Let the Dead Bury the Dead!!!

Throughout history, spiritual leaders have counseled that we will never be able to evolve to a higher state of consciousness or create a human society based on health, happiness, love, peace, and success, until we give up the brutal habit of eating meat. A vegetarian diet is an ideal diet for the African man. When eaten fresh and uncooked, raw fruits and vegetables in the proper combinations and quantities will provide all of the elements of health needed by the body.

Raw fruits and vegetables have plenty of plant proteins, carbohydrates, fats, minerals, and vitamins which are of the highest quality. Fruits and vegetables also supply the purest form of water for human consumption. This was a normal diet for people of Africa. No wonder they lived for hundreds of years, free from disease. The Ancient Africans built some of the greatest empires known to man: Egyptian, Mali, Songhai, Jenné, Timbuktu, Ethiopian, and Gao, just to name a few.

The Africans or Blacks in America are the descendants of these great people of antiquity. Diet played an important role in their strength, endurance, their ability to get along with each other, along with working in harmony with nature. Everybody and Everything have its Purpose. We as Human Beings, Transforming into Spiritual Beings (God-Like) must find out its Reason for Existing. "Seek And Ye Shall Find!!!" Always Remember That It Is What It Is!!! Learn!

Our organism will not permanently put up with our violations against nature; it simply becomes more and more impaired. Impairments, whether from disease or from surgery, always effect the whole body in many ways. The following is the chain of effects: lowering of the vital energy of the organism; slowed function of bodily processes; accumulation of waste products; acute and chronic disease; and death. If only we would put forth as much effort to obey Nature's Laws, as the Ancient Africans who are the ancestors of African-Americans. Since African-Americans have adopted the erroneous ways of Euro-Americans, they are busy putting a lot of energy in finding ways to violate nature, or escape the consequences of our disobedience to it. Unfortunately, our violations and escapism lead only to imprisonment of a sick body. Diseases are more popular than anything: Heart Attacks, Ebola, Flu Virus, Aids, Autism, Breast Cancer, Prostate Cancer, Colon Cancer, Ovarian Cancer, and etc., etc.. Diseases Only Produces More Diseases!! Knowledge of Oneself is the Only Key!!!

We may seem clever at giving a specific drug treatment, or at robbing vital energy from one area of the body and forcing it to another, but the organism cannot be tricked or triggered into health. Drugs and treatments are not cures (causes of healing) anymore than germs are the causes of illness, or that illness is the cause of pain and death. These are ignorant beliefs developed by Euro-American doctors and scientists for the sole purpose of keeping you sick; to take your money, and as a result, you will never deal with the causes. Instead, you will continuously and blindly fight effects. We must keep in mind that doctors in America are trained to push drugs or medicine and deal with effects and symptoms.

It is very strange that drugs or medicines, substances that weaken the strong and well, are given to the weak and ill. The short-term relief from symptoms and the so-called power of cure mistakenly attributed to drugs, surgery, supplements, herbs, and etc. are never worth the long-term losses, emotionally, mentally or spiritually. In truth, we survive in spite of drugs and treatments, not because of them.

Commitment does not always create being comfortable with your efforts. Remember that doing the right thing is not always comfortable. We must continue to fight for our right to be the person we need to be. Can you keep on moving (Growing and Learning) while you are hurting? Accept the challenge because you are always blessed through your efforts (Action). Keep on Learning from Your Choices and Be Wiser! The true answer (only answer that is the light to see your way clear) is always to be sought. Sometimes it is hard to find. You must be persistent in your efforts because if you keep on seeking, then you will eventually find!

How Much Do You Believe In Your Efforts!!! Transition and everything else that comes along with it begins in the mind (Man). All transition has a starting point and the desired destination. Be clear and be aware.

What is essential for the creation of an organism is also essential for its growth and preservation. Fresh air, pure water, food (raw fruits and vegetables, seeds and nuts in the correct quantity and combination), worship, sleep, exercise, sunshine, cleanliness - these are just a few of the known essentials to be used with love, positive thoughts and feelings which were natural to the Africans of Antiquity. To be lacking in any one essential is to live contrary to nature. This has been shown by the negative results, which always follow the American way of life. Essentials are impossible to duplicate in a laboratory, and they do not require the slaughter of animals or the use of their products, which is so prevalent in American society. It is pitiful to say that 70% or more of all products in the supermarkets have some form of the animal ingredient in it.

Fasting is the most powerful of all tools for cleansing the body. Most people ingest as part of their diet preservatives, insecticides, lead, arsenic, medication, nicotine, and caffeine.

Their bodies accumulate toxic waste products from wrong and/or badly combined food, and from excessive eating. This is a normal, everyday way of life in America. Capitalism breeds this style of degradation and dehumanizing ways, which is an attitude of "get as much as you can," by any means necessary. Instead of harmonizing with one another and nature, it causes competition and greed, a dog-eat-dog attitude.

Beware of all the agencies that were and are created to deceive us, just to control us and take our money, making people economic slaves. People become very dependent on those who don't give a damn about you (no jobs, welfare, no or rotten education, stealing children: DHS, more prisons, more hospitals, and etc.).

The fasting person benefits morally because by fasting, he learns that he should be prepared to suffer the greatest sacrifice and undergo (transform) the hardest trial rather than indulge in that which is not permitted to him by his own choice in order to grow. The body has a limited capacity to eliminate this toxic load. When the accumulation starts to interfere with proper function, the body sends out warnings such as aches, pains and the visible signs of the disorder. It is time for the Black man in America to do some serious housecleaning. Our Creator will not enter into a house (Mind) that is filthy. We have to start renewing our minds toward our natural way of life: Right Thinking; Right Giving; and Right Eating.

## The Mind

The mind is your highest state of consciousness. It is also the overseer, controls habits, and it must be disciplined in order to control our thoughts and actions. Your mind is the center of your will power. Dr. Haile Baba, Priest-King of the Nation of Alkebulan, states that "You should never use your will power without first having understanding, or you are headed for destruction." African-Americans, by nature, have a strong will power, but they lack the first ingredient, which is understanding. The Bible even states, "...Above all your getting, get understanding." Dr. Haile Baba farther stated that, "It has always been one of the most difficult practical problems to present the truth so as not to offend those who are ingrained with old errors."

Don't only go through life, Grow Through Life. Stick-to-itiveness is unwavering pertinacity. Perseverance as the elders and ancestors have always said and demonstrated that we need some stick-to-itiveness in order to get ahead (progress). Too often we have projects and never finish them. The results will be too much-unfinished business without closing them, which can produce no more room for anything else. In order to add projects, you would have to either finish, close them down, or eliminate some of them, if not all of them, to make room for the new. Some people feel that they can hold on to things that have become stale and rotten, while they are adding new things in their lives. You must get rid of the old to make room for the new. If you don't, you are setting yourself up with frustration, anger, giving up, depression, high emotions. and being unfair to yourself and all others, with no just cause. You see it all the time. We must find a way to rotate, rearrange, cleanup and cleanout, which produces change, so that we can keep on moving with a lighter and more clear path. Change You Must! Self Preservation again is the key to keeping and developing your Balance. Life Is Balance! So, therefore, we must take heed and respect the realities of Life.Keep on learning and keep on growing, you can't go wrong. Life has no respect of person, it will work for you if you are obedient to Its Laws.

## *People Power*

Life gives to those who give to it accordingly. Life does not care how or what you feel because Life does not deal with feelings or emotions. Life loves and will give to those who give to it. Keep in mind that you can not manipulate, change, fool, or disrespect it. Doing that will result in disastrous results that you can not prepare for because Life is Life. Learn and cooperate and be blessed. It will keep you in perfect peace whose mind is stayed on thee.

Life is good, fair, and merciful to those who are in tune with it. Put your feelings in your back pocket and get the job done, in Divine Order! Much cooperation is necessary. Remember to always do what is necessary, no matter what or how you feel. Feelings are a human thing. Life is a mental and spiritual thing. So, step up to the plate and hit a grand slam for the Team-Your People. Be a Team player and you can never go wrong, no matter how things seem. Use your God given senses correctly and you will always have divine results from The Most High. Life will always reward those who believe in it. Most people don't believe what they believe! Check them out and you will see for yourself. As soon as the challenge come, look at how they fall apart and eventually give up and give in. The ones before us laid the foundation to a Divine Way of Life. What are we looking for when all we have to do is seek, find, and follow. There is nothing new under the Sun. They were wise and understanding towards life. You will really know something when you see the difference. A discerning Spirit is a Must. Know The Differences!

The first lesson that the Ancient Africans (a purely religious and spiritual people) taught was the establishment of a positive attitude within yourself is essential. Establishing self-confidence and self-reliance frees you of the dreaded fears that you probably consciously or unconsciously harbor. Africans, who were brought to America against their will to be slaves, are existing in a system of a disease-ridden society beget by grief, worry, nagging insecurity, life-sapping influences and premature death, and most of them are not aware or concerned. Know Thyself! If you know yourself, then you know who God is!

Dr. Haile Baba developed a superior program to raise the consciousness of the African-Americans:

"Your social environment is critical to your health and happiness. I want to re-emphasize that your social environment is largely what made you. Much of my teachings are involved with reprogramming yourself! Most of this is in reorienting your attitude and values. By becoming aware of your great powers, you will be well down the road to mastering yourself and your environment so that you harness these wondrous powers in your behalf - and in behalf of your nation."

Self-examination should be a daily process of each

person. Take time to get an honest inventory of your conditioned mental thoughts. Using your thought process, at the end of the day, ask yourself how your day went. Do you feel the need of changing your mental attitude in order to feel better? Be honest with yourself. In many cultures, America included, worry and an erroneous diet are considered a sign of affluence, security, and an alright-with-me symbol. But, we must remember that nature is just! She demands obedience to her laws. Eventually, we are penalized if we double-cross her, but we are always rewarded if we obey her. She is always on our side.

In the beginning, your faith may not be strong enough to motivate you to action, but the closer you come to proper attitudes and obedience in your worship of the Creator, the stronger that faith becomes. Soon it will be strong enough to light up your life and motivate you to do good deeds and works. Do Not Give Up, No Matter How It Seems. All is a Part of the Process! Are you willing?

All living organisms are self-directing, self-constructing, self-defending, self-preserving, self-maintaining, and in the event of injury or illness, self-repairing or self-healing. Knowing your tremendous inner capabilities frees you of many burdensome illusions and provides a key to true life enchantment. "Tis better to be ignorant than to know so much that isn't so," says a philosopher. Every person is responsible for themselves. Your mind and body are always on Trial. "Know thyself," says the Ancients of Africa. Only the truth (The Light) can and will set you free from ignorance. We must continue to learn how to become a light (Truth). Study to Show Yourself Approved.

Humans are creatures of habits: good, bad, and indifferent. Habits are conditioned responses, which we rely upon for personal efficiency. We spent many years from infant-hood on learning resonances and procedures to many thousands of situations and circumstances. When situations reoccur, we almost or wholly unconsciously employ our habit patterns. Most of African-Americans habits are learned from others who learned from yet others, back into slavery and ignorance.

Habits are always adapted and employed in accord with our own peculiar programming: mass psychology. There is no wonder the African-Americans are confused and either being destroyed or destroying themselves or both. Since Africans have their own history, culture, language, tradition and religion, it would be very destructive to totally adapt someone else way of life. Could this be the situation of the Africans in America? Eagles pretending or learning how to be something that they are not-chickens and pigeons. Never depend on another kind of bird to show and teach you how to be an Eagle that soars above them all, and sometimes have them for breakfast, lunch, or dinner. Learn how to be what you were created to be The Greatest Of All. Believe That!

Only a fool would think that a people who denied another people the opportunity to live like a decent human being, enslaved your fore-parents, oppressed, mocked and scorned your people, would trust you with some "grand secrets." Africans in America have been made to live under the heat of Hatred and Oppression. We have been distressed every since we were forced here in America. Keep Up The Fight For Your Freedom! Any Means Necessary!! We have everything to gain!!!

Habits are wonderful, for they are the foundation upon which our advanced human attainments have been built. The key to a successful and happy life is to build your habits around your ancestor's culture. Thus, it follows that we are no better and can perform no better than the limitation of our programming. It is unfortunate, but no accident, that all African-Americans are incorrectly attuned to a greater or lesser extent in many of their life programs.

Dr. Haile Baba states that "We (Africans) are fortunate in that we, like computers, can be re-programmed for better performance and more rewarding results. We are grateful for our indigenous religion (belief system). If our capabilities are equal to 100 on a scale of potential, it is said that we do not achieve more than 5 to 10. We only fractionally use our thinking ability. We have become the creatures of habit."

Circumstances, situations, and people of all levels will no doubt challenge your identity. Preparation is the key! First and foremost, we must know thyself, which is the first law of any individual's life. Keep in mind that life is Order and Balance. Total cooperation of God's laws is definitely necessary.

Mind is above and beyond the physical-metaphysical. It is a stream of consciousness, intelligent, creativeness, flowing in and through us from the Creative Force. Bach gives steps in understanding mind: mind exists in every cell of the body; mind is innate wisdom; mind is anatomical brain; mind is intuitive; mind is super-conscious, and mind is universal.

"As spirit, mind, and body are inseparable, so are exercise, nutritional eating and fasting. They work together and complement one another holistically."

We must act on truth always. Always remember that everything takes a process, good or bad. We have to develop an attitude to learn. The only thing that can remove a force is another force that has greater power. In order for a person to rule in falsehood, he must first know the truth to create a lie (illusion).

There is a need for discipline: self-disciple. No other discipline is of lasting value. Undisciplined desires rule and ruin millions. Uncontrolled desires are like runaway teams, they smash things up. Appetites and passions are in need of discipline; emotions require discipline. Dr.

Haile Baba beautifully says that, "In all things, we need to discipline ourselves to the highest and best in life," for the benefit of the nation.

Discipline means much more than a code of "thou shalt nots..." It must include all of the attitudes of life, everything pertaining to a pattern of product that tends to lift us up to a higher and more desirable plane of living, for the Africans in America and around the world. It is not wise to make the most of the many delicious and wholesome things that we can eat, in partaking of those things; it must be in moderation by using restraints. We must let our ideals take the place of the restraints. When we have done this, the restraints cease to be restraints.

If you are determined to make your life and your way of life really amount to something, you will not fail to rise above every obstacle that stands in your way. Never look at a complex problem as complex. It can cause you to exaggerate the problem to the point that you talk your way out of addressing it properly. Everything takes a process and we must learn the process before approaching the problem so that you will at least know what is expected of your efforts. Be prepared for the unexpected. Develop Reserve!!

Always factor in the possibilities. When you factor in the possibilities, that does not make you negative as some say you are out of jealousy and hate. It prepares you to have the things that you also know that could happen, especially dealing with people who you know, that don't have their balance. When you factor that in, it will soften up the sting if anything presents itself, so that you can have enough to keep on going to fulfill your purpose. There is nothing that is more important than your Purpose. If not, it can and will overwhelm you to the point that you will misread and give up and give in. Factoring in the possibilities before you go headlong into a situation will cause you to approach a person or situation carefully. Be full of care for your own Balance. In other words, "To Thine Own Self Be True."

Once you recognize your body's inherent power to heal itself; you can get with the task of changing your mental-physical habits and create your own living sculpture: your body. The body and mind are one. In truth, the mind, body, and all faculties are an integrated and inseparable unit. Looking at an individual as a double or triple entity of body, mind, and spirit (soul) is completely wrong. Remember, "You are 98% mental and spiritual, and 2% physical" stated Dr. Haile Baba.

There is balance with everything that is about life. You just cannot do what you want to do. Only balance can bring you successful results. We must be willing and prepared to make sacrifices to reach successful results. Something big does not come without a big fight (inner and outer forces). One has to be tuned into the truth because that is all that matters.

# *People Power*

The role of your subconscious mind (your body intelligence) is to take orders from your conscious mind. In order to let your subconscious determine your living practices, you need to clean your mental house of all negative tendencies and contradictory beliefs. If your conscious mind is filled with contradictory beliefs, you will give your subconscious mind opposite orders, such as orders for health and sickness at the same time. For instances, you desire health, but your concepts are for sickness.

Such contradictory orders interfere with the bodily intellectual ability to create health. You can see the results of such contrary beliefs in the habits of the general populace, especially African-Americans. All individuals desire health and happiness, and yet most people indulge in eating junk foods, drinking alcohol, taking drugs, flesh-eating (meat), smoking and eating dairy products, all of which depress the organism towards sickness. Everyone is in effect saying, "I want health-sickness." All sicknesses are diseases (not at ease). Ignorance of self is the father of deterioration.

The first Law of Nature is also knowing yourself. You will continue to fail until you learn and practice the first Law of Life. Keep in mind that we have been tricked into believing lies and deception which caused us to be against our individual selves and each other. Because of that, you will approach Life with eyes that have many veils of illusions, which caused us many hellish results. Can you imagine a person or people going through life avoiding the first Law of Life, which is Self-Preservation?

Too many of us are on that road of distruction. We need to wake up and get to know and learn about the man in the mirror. I know that it can be scary, but man up and woman up and get to know yourself to start loving and respecting yourself. Let us build courage and face the truth about our personal reality. Never allow anyone to challenge you more than you challenge yourself. The ones who intentionally, deliberately, and willfully avoid challenging themselves, are qualified to be in the catagory of being a coward.

That's Right! How can you know yourself if you never or some times challenge yourself? You Can't. Facing your reality can be very painful, hurting, and uncomfortable, but you must find a way, everybody has to find their way to a divine way of Life. Everyone has an obligation to find themselves and adjust accordingly. You can do it my people! Why would you always challenge and critique others and refuse to do that with yourself. Respect, Love, and Know Thyself, first and foremost.

Have Courage and never let yourself down! We got in this mess together and we must come out of it together with respect first, and then build Love. That is Order! We need each other more than ever before. Team effort is the goal!!

## *People Power*

Your body is your own living sculpture and the results you see are the results of your own conscious creative abilities. To change from sickness towards health, you must go to work like the artist that works with clay.

Use the conscious mind to create a goal; a finished sculpture. Your goal will be a youthful, healthy body and by consciously striving to create a healthy body, you will make contact with your own inner resources. By keeping within your conscious mind a picture of your goal, a youthful, healthy body, you will be less likely to indulge in unhealthy habits. This life goal insures our survival as an African people, and can only be achieved when you invest your life with the elements and influences necessary to produce them.

Our African Ancestors, of antiquity's way of life, presents a system of healthful living that is 100% effective delivering health and longevity. The system embraces all that bears upon their well-being. It is fundamentally in accord with every requirement of their human heritage.

As long as we continue to be economic slaves (trapped) to our ways (created by our conscious or unconscious bad attitudes), we will continue to create the results that are happening in our communities. These results are: Disrespect for one another; Police brutality; DHS stealing our children; Welfare buying the souls of our women; who in return sell the souls of our children for a trinket; Depending on the government agents; Being non-cultural, by not knowing who and who's you are, and so on. The enemies of our life, which has always been white supremacy and ignorance, have caused African-Americans to be born injured, wounded, confused, disconnected, and overly emotional, disrespected and looked down on, and so on.

Africans had always understood the laws that govern the universe; such as the Law of Karma, and it's effect on life. The word "Karma" is the hidden term for cause and effect, or you reap what you sow; what goes around comes around; what you see is what you get. This law completely determines everything that occurs in our lives, both inner development and outer development. It is through the application of this law that we make or break our lives, even though we may not be aware of this. School yourself and don't fool yourself. It is through an understanding of what this law entails, that we are able to make our life into what it should be. Sometimes (most of the time), the truth is too incredible to bare. That is why most people rebel and get angry

It seems like the more simple that Life is, the more suspicious we become because we are so use to things being difficult. Remember, the scripture says that life is Simplicity. The simple things in Life are the most important. So, take it easy, nice and slow! In other words, make every move you make and every step you take count! Start right now because you can do it.

# People Power

## The Spirit

Most people allow their personal feelings to determine how they respond. Feelings (emotions) can cause you not to see things correctly. It can blind you to reality and cause you to create illusions that are only real to you. According to what you believe, it is real to you, so be mindful of what you believe. In reality, most people don't believe what they believe. That is why they are unstable and constantly changing their position and as a result, they become a contradiction and a hypocrite. Be still and know that the Truth is always what matters. It is the Light that causes you to see, and the more you see, the more accurate and just you will be in your approach to the situation. Always judge by Righteous judgment. In other words, be fair and true. Turn your Lights on (mental and spiritual) and keep them bright because we are in a world that deals in illusions.

Too many meta-physicians believe that karma pertains only to the unpleasant things that happen to us, but it also brings us blessings that we have when we have the proper understanding of the Law of Karma. It is through this law that we come to the realization that as divine spiritual beings, as Ancient Africans taught, we alone are responsible for the good or evil that we encounter. It also makes us realize that the Creator never punishes us. You did not make yourself all by yourself; it took friends, parents, teachers, deceitful preachers, and government agencies, to help create all the causes you have created. African-Americans and Africans throughout the world need to join an organized structure to undo the negative causes and help each other to create positive causes. The Nation of Alkebulan, Nation of Islam, Hebrew Israelite, Yoruba, Nubian-Hebrew-Islamic Community, and United Negro Improvement Association (UNIA) are a few of the positive, organized structured Black African organizations that were organized and practiced by African-Americans.

"We realize from this law that whatever the problem may be that discomforts us, it is not something that has happened by accident," says Dr. Haile Baba. We created it. Nothing just happens by accident, everything that happens is just. "The sun does not rise by accident. There is a reason for it to rise." Everything is in Divine Order. Get in the flow! Everything has a cause, whether we realize it or not. It makes us realize that we are the creators of what happens in our lives, and the Creator never punishes us. We punish ourselves by not understanding this law of cause and effect - Karma. The Bible's teachings are based on this law from Genesis to Revelations.

The understanding that Mind has caused man to be what man really is - the Creator's image, likeness, and reflection, releases us from the bondage of material heredity; it sets us free to prove our real identity as the witness of God.

"People of African Ancestry have a natural life span of 1,000 years or more. "We can live this long without any sickness whatsoever, if their biological mandate is observed," says Dr. Haile Baba. The Bible even states that people of Genesis, were begetting babies at eight-hundred and nine-hundred years old.

In reality, all healing is self-healing. Nothing in the world outside of the body faculties has the power and intelligence to assess body problems, and to create the cells and fluids necessary to effect tissue repair. What is normally preferred to as "healing" is unnecessary in the lives of the healthy. Restoration of health is only in those who have lost their health. We doubt ourselves, which causes us to never reach our destination of transforming into our Godhood (Being Like Our Father: The Creator). Righteous people are being made when no one else is watching. The Revolution Will Not Be Televised! Self Preservation Always!!

Health can be regained and maintained only by healthful living. All that is introduced into or on the body, other than those essentials, normal and natural, to the body, is harmful.

People of African Ancestry are naturally good, altruistic and kind, and will exhibit their virtuous nature if the conditions normal to their existence are established. That is why it is necessary and a must for us to come together as one, to develop a program that would enhance a healthy lifestyle, for the purpose of a superior people, that once existed.

Today, our children observe our behavior and have lost the natural respect and love for us and themselves. What do we expect from them, other than that which they have become, fashioned and shaped by our hands as we participate in their destruction? Another generation is growing up and we as a people, as a whole, have not changed our behavior for the good. There are not many positive images for our children. We even send them to schools that are not relevant; schools that do not teach them the knowledge of self and kind. They are taught inferior education, to love and respect everyone except themselves, which leads them to destruction. Consequently, the problem that plagues our communities if not properly dealt with will cause the loss of many lives. If we fail to come to our children's aid now, how will history view us later?

Will it say that we did not have the patience or capacity to take charge of our obligations and responsibilities? We need to re-establish our cultural scientists, which are the mothers of our children: The First Teacher; The Master Teacher!!!

Toxic materials must be very low in the blood stream and the body before the brain can function at maximum efficiency. The brain is a phenomenal instrument of 50 billion nerve cells and nerve fibers seeking to control, but also responds to the undisciplined whims and wishes of the body. Nothing beclouds our minds so much as toxemia or toxicosis. Even a bloodstream laden with the intake of nutrients from a meal will cause the mind to perform less efficiently than if the meal had not been eaten. It has been well said that a full stomach makes a dull head.

Fasting is known to be the oldest cause for the cure of the body and mind. When we undergo a fast, there is vastly accelerated body and blood cleansing. There is noticeable regeneration of physical faculties. There is great enhancement of nerve energy. The body does a general housecleaning and overall of the whole economy. Thus, we can see the wisdom of the traditional forty day fast as practiced by our African Ancestors.

Researchers and Dr. Haile Baba's revelations reveal that people seem to learn faster when hungry, and to rate higher in intelligence tests when hungry than when the stomach is full. An African proverb says, "A full stomach does not like to think." This well expresses a fact that is known to all mental workers and good students. A full meal leaves them dull, unable to think clearly and continuously, and often makes them stupid and sleepy. Mental workers have learned to eat a light breakfast and lunch, and have their heavy meal in the evening after the day's work is done. This is contrary to the American way. Could this be one of the problems, why people have a tendency to have a slow thinking capacity in the morning and afternoon? It takes a lot of energy to digest the American breakfast and lunch, especially if meat is consumed.

Why should fasting result in an increase in mental abilities? Primarily, because it affords the body an opportunity to throw off its load of toxins; hence the brain is fed by cleaner blood. Secondarily, the rest of all the functions of life is enhanced by fasting because it supplies the brain with more power to think. Euro-American ways of life tends to dull the mental powers; especially with their nationally drug addictions and their almost universal overeating which tend to reduce mental abilities.

We must separate the bad of ourselves for the good. We must be able and willing to identify the bad that we are entertaining and carrying along with ourselves and the corruption that we are willfully accepting in our own individual life. Identify and separate from it. We must be able to distinguish the corrupt behavior in our communities, and separate ourselves from the corrupt ones, and then the good ones can band together and meet, and face the bad influences and actions that destroys us and our future children, who are our future leaders and soldiers of the light (Truth).

Dr. Haile Baba calls attention to the fact that people of African ancestry practice of fasting be universally observed today. "What a wonderful world this would be. We wouldn't have so many low grade mentalities around getting married, divorced, and dying, in a false culture for us." We could see the error and dehumanizing, degenerating effects of family.

Poverty (economic slavery) is a huge artificial restraint in our communities. Beware of devaluing our progress by being overly concerned about people, those who are not in the flow of life for us as a people. We have to stop sawing the saw dust. The unwanted and unneeded tree should be sawed down for good. We can do it! Always be patient with yourself because your efforts through time will yield a great harvest!!

Intellectual pursuits use more mental energy than physical labor. Thinking draws more current from our mental batteries than digging ditches. No doubt you've seen people become physically exhausted without doing a lick of physical work. You can witness this in meetings where people sit and discuss and contend.

To build a nation, there must never be discord, but dictatorship with love. The stresses of intellectual contention are enough in themselves, in many cases to short circuit or drain our reserves of nerve energy. One reason why, is that there are not enough real beneficial Black organizations or Black nations.

A man (mind or thinker) that can't manage his own mind is a man that is given to foolishness. He is given to irregularity and is not consistent in goodness, but once a man (thinker) is able to manage his own mind, he then lives a consistently good life. That is the trouble with the Western world. The West (government) has sensitized the people, the subjects or citizens to do everything but manage their own minds. In fact, the thing that is feared most is the individual taking upon himself the responsibility of his own mind. The first law of nature: "Self Preservation". No One Is Exempt!!!

Dr. Haile Baba contends that, "I've seen people rise in heated discussion and be like a dynamo with plenty of intellectual energy. I've seen people in intense emotional states lapse into a state of depression. Many people call this nervous exhaustion. I call it enervation, meaning very simply, without nerve energy." We must open our eyes to stress before we can have the nerve energy to deal with an organized lifestyle based on our African family structures.

People of African Ancestry have become a nation of stimulant hounds. We take on stimulating drinks like coffee and sodas, heated discussions, and many of us smoke. We take on stimulating seasoned foods; that is food which the body rejects. That which stimulates is stuff that irritates. So, we get an artificial perk up; we thereby further drain our nerve energy.

That's the way it works in and on us, but these stimulant habits also drain us of brain power. Stimulants makes us mentally more acute for a short time, but then we must face depression, and a much lower mental state. Brain damage to some extent invariably results. One bad thing begets another, and that is the other side of what I was saying above; bad conditions beget worst conditions. Worse conditions eventually lead to ailments and diseases that further lower you mentally.

You must turn yourself around by exercising, eating right, and fasting. Next to fasting for mental acuity, it is essential to develop good eating habits by means of selecting proper, wholesome foods that were originally created for our consumption. Actually, our goal in claiming a right to holistic health lies in understanding what reality is now. To know man's present, indestructible relationship to the Creator, the source of all wholeness and health, assures us of our perfect self-hood. We will rise into more consistently health-filled lives. Many people are losing their passion for life by many poor or incorrect choices which cause poor results. Love and respect yourself and your people (those who acknowledge Truth).

So let's begin and then continue to exercise our divine right to health. This is our rightful inheritance as total-beings.

Many are called, but few are chosen. If you don't qualify yourself, then you will never be chosen by Our Father or by Our Family (Ancestors). We must give each other  reason to be there for one another. The harvest is plentiful, but the laborers are fewer than ever before. Don't be deceived that just because you are here that you automatically will be chosen. Everything in Life is earned, good or bad-Cause and Effect. Let us all qualify ourselves to be a part of the Spiritual Family in order to protect ourselves from the evil forces. You will be blessed many times over-100 Fold. Let the spirits of our Ancestors lead, guide, and direct us to a Heavenly Lifestyle. Try it, you will definitely thank Our Creator for our blessed results. Know that, everyone is blessed through their individual efforts. Don't let yourself down because many have and many will.

## NOTES

## NOTES

# Chapter III

# Family

Perhaps the most important realization that comes to us through the law of cause and effect (Karma) is the fact that in reality, there is only one problem we have to solve, and that problem is personal relationships with our individual self and each other. For our own life reflects the results of our actions and reactions to others. We must remember that all choices have a future that is correlated.

Family as defined by the laws of nature and the universe is when two or more fractions or functional units come together for the sake of perpetuating their kind at a mental, physical and spiritual level more evolved than the existing structure. The primary goals and objectives, mission, task and purpose for coming together is for continuation thru regeneration of a like life form of a higher order than the existing structure; and in that coming together the spiritual energy as well as the physical characteristics and mental order of the initiating forces are given renewed life as often as the birth cycle can occur within the harmony of nature and the universe.

We find today that so-called black leaders have been concentrating on all institutions except for the most important - family. The Pan-African Federation Organization, founded and organized by Dr. Edward Robinson, Calvin Robinson, and Redman Battles, has taught for years that Blacks (Africans) have had seven veils of illusions to trick them up. These veils being: education, politics, jobs, money, housing, economics, and religion. However, these illusions are not just to trick Blacks, but to trick up a specific institution in the lives of the Blacks: being the family. These illusions have been marched for; died for; preached for; and begged for with each revealing that it isn't the answer to the disunity of the Black (African) community. Even considering racism, which the Euro-Americans perpetuate against the Africans in America, will not penetrate when and only when the Black (African) family is unified. Historically, we find that the African Nations of Antiquity were built from the center, which is the family. With the nucleus being the family, which was the strongest institution in the nation, it was the foundation that created all societies. When a man (thinker) does not know who he is, he does not know what belongs to him, or he does not know how to get it.

Other people (forces, energies) manipulated us from a position that we were and are unaware of. We must develop an attitude to learn. We must learn the art of learning. Yes, learning is an art skill. First, we must be about gathering information, and when you internalize the information, then it becomes knowledge. Once you become knowledgeable, then you must be able to comprehend and master the information by studying and/or experiencing. We must always keep in mind that today's school systems understand the significance of arts and sciences that is part of the makeup for all of African descent. In other words, we as a people can not do without arts and sciences. So know that there is a conspiracy in the American school systems to deliberately discontinue teaching arts and sciences that African-American nature needs. We cannot do without them!

We have developed our belief systems based on these skills. That is why the average African-American does not excel in the American school systems because we as people will always feel a void without these skills. The system knows, and they understand that. The system knows us very well. Any time a thing or person is missing a link in life, then the children can not function properly. It will produce children that will be off balance. Anything or person that is not balanced will eventually fall or break. That person(s) is headed for a lot of serious negative consequences, such as mental illness, physically unhealthy, and not even born spiritually. If your mind is not right, then everything else in your life affairs will not be right.

Mind is everything!

Balance is the key to keeping you to stay upright. Since Euro Americans know that, they developed institutions to perpetuate their games of creating illusions of what balance is for African-Americans. How can a chicken teach an Eagle how to be, act, and look like an Eagle even though both are birds? They are different kinds of birds that have their own unique way of life. You will find out that everything ain't for everybody. Beware of the magicians and illusionist! In other words, everything and everybody you see are not necessarily what it appears to be.

Keep on learning and keep on growing because you can not go wrong. Study to show yourself approval. Independent study, outside of the school system will cause you to learn things that are necessary to live a righteous life. Always ask questions for clarification. Do not be afraid to ask. Never take things or people for face value, because all is more than the eyes can see.

To Know Self Is To Know God and Visa Versa. This is also included in the First Law of Nature. Cheikh Anta Diop, in his most profound book, <u>The Cultural Unity of Black Africa</u> stated:

"The reconstruction of the history of family is uncovered into four main types:

(1)    The oldest, which arose out of the primitive state of promiscuous intercourse, is the family which

is said to be consanguine: it is marked by the fact that marriage is only forbidden between parents and their children.

(2)   The second is the punaluan family. It is a whole group of sisters or of cousins, which will be wed by a group of brothers or cousins outside their circle.

(3)   The third form is the pairing family, this is a monogamy with mutual facilities for divorce. This was the type which existed throughout Indian society.

(4)   The fourth type is the monogamous patriarchal family where divorce is rendered if not impossible, at least extremely difficult, where the woman lives in total dependency on her husband and is legally subjected to him."

Today, this unit called family has been the key that has opened the door for people who have been subjected to the worst form of slavery, in the history of the world; the enslavement of Black Africans by Europeans or Caucasians. All that was allowed was a fragmented unit called a family. In this day and time, we find the same conditions, a fragmented unit. As a result, the father, even though not being sold to another plantation, is absent due to a lack of cooperation from his wife, or due to his own irresponsibility. We find children who are not physically or mentally created to deny their parent's existence, but who want to be so "grown" and independent, that they leave home in search of something better. However, we find one thing that has not changed, and that is the same wicked tricks, of the oppressor, creating chaos between African-Americans; the same divide and conquer tactics. Every institution that is created in America, causes disunity in the Black (African) family.

It is the Caucasian mentality of the Black man that causes havoc in our communities. It is time for the Black man to get his Mind in Divine Order (Balance) to better our conditions, but we have to qualify ourselves through various tests (challenges and opportunities). Understand that everything will take a specific and significant process. Being open-minded and very flexible mentally, by always factoring in the possibilities, is very much necessary. Life requires that amount of willingness. We must act on Truth!

History tells us that Black African people were kidnapped and brought to America against their will, and built a wealthy society, with free labor. Can you imagine the horroristic mental effect that slavery not only took on the Ancient Africans, but also on their children, which today are the African-Americans? All children must be taught where they come from, what happened to their ancestors, and what direction they should be going. This will bring about an understanding of their history, culture, tradition, and language, which will create dignity and pride within themselves.

# *People Power*

Black people in America have been mis-educated to the point that they don't even get any justice from her. We have become suicidal in our ways because of our mis-education. We must surrender ourselves to our Creator and our Ancestors who were given the blueprint of life by our Creator. Always remember that in order to tell a lie, you must first know the truth. We must learn and then act on Truth!!! Mystery only means that you missed the story. Once you know the story, you know the truth.

With the African family structure being slowed or destroyed during slavery, but in some cases still practiced, it gave them a sense of belonging, and therefore a sense of security in the adverse conditions they were in. However, the master seeing this situation, began at once to totally destroy the family structure. As a result, he sold the man (husband) to another plantation, and the children to even another plantation, leaving the woman (wife and mother) alone; which all three experienced a horroristic mental effect. Today are the results which created confusion.

This was a normal condition created by the "slave master" against the indigenous Africans who were kidnapped and brought to America to build a wealthy society for the Europeans. They also stole this land from the indigenous Western Indians and from some of the Blacks who were already here before slavery. Yes, there were plenty of Blacks here before slavery. Once again, study to show yourself approved. Your study has to be done independently, which is not a requirement from the American institutions which are not designed for African-Americans. Seek and you shall find!

Should these vicious and cruel acts done by European (Caucasian) people, be called civilized people?

History has a purpose, which is to test man with the Truth he himself chooses to accept. Anyone who can tolerate or accept poverty becomes automatically ignorant and poor in many ways. Anytime we suffer, it starts from the inside out. We must become practitioners, instead of being reactors. Thought creates your circumstances and your behavior. Attitude is the key to your thoughts and feelings. Life will definitely work for those who work with it. We must understand that life does not care how you feel. In fact, life does not deal with feelings or emotions. Life is based on your actions and deeds, which are determined by what you know and believe. According to your beliefs, it is done unto you. So, be careful with what you believe because it will manifest in your life.

Everyone is accountable for what they know and what they believe. Most people find out that they know very little about Life, and that they eventually don't believe what they believe. They have become very hypocritical and a contradiction to themselves. That usually results in being very frustrated and confused. When a person knows and believes something, you should see evidence of it consistently. The proof is in the putting (action). If you don't see evidence, then don't believe the hype, no matter who it is. If you see evidence, then believe it, good or bad. It is not always who it is, but it is always What it is! Be true to yourself and keep it Real.

We find that this society whose control, presently is in the hands of the offspring of the slave master, has always concentrated on keeping the Black (African) family down or under control. During slavery, as Lawrence W. Levin states in his book, <u>Black Culture and Black Consciousness</u> that the slaves were even beaten for talking about identifying with a family.

"I was once whipped, a freed man in New Orleans told David Macrea, because I said to Misses, my mother sent me. We were not allowed to call our mammies, mother." Any group that was potentially cohesive because of family was deliberately divided or tightly controlled to prevent unity. Know your history (our story).

To establish or redevelop an African family structure, using ancient culture as a frame of reference, is the first major step toward positive regeneration of mind, body and spiritual development, and of re-establishing ones natural flow in harmony with the creative force - God. The first basic step is to eliminate the adverse affects through the re-establishment of self love, self discipline, and self respect. Also the re-establishment of one's mental, physical, and spiritual role in life as defined by the Creator of universal order.

Think, for surely thoughtfulness is resourceful. It has great benefit and the most powerful in resourcefulness to produce for you in the thinking of our Creator. How is the thinking on our Creator going to be resourceful and productive? If you do not know how to form a proper relationship with our Creator, then one cannot benefit from anything. We must build a firm relationship first with our individual self. Once you know who you are, then you will know who our Creator is, says our Ancestors. "Seek And Ye Shall Find."

African-Americans, today have been programmed, psyched and hypnotized into being something contrary to their nature, by a people (Caucasians) who despise their existence. In most cases, the male and female roles have been switched. The Black (African) woman have been tricked into being the dominant force of the two, which is contrary to their family structure. She is no longer dependent on the man, but is in essence dependent on the white system. The welfare system, has been set up to keep this dependency in force. Therefore, the Black female depended on this system, and as a result the Black man could not be her man. This brings about a financially independent attitude in the Black female which she now brags, "I don't need no man, I can make it on my own." The Black males are also programmed to believe that he doesn't need to build a family because of the availability of a surplus of females. In most cases, even if the family is together, there is disunity. A unit of this nature tends to move in opposition of natural order. Everyone tends to eat whatever they wish or desire, whenever they wish or desire; or tend to eat of the same negative structure and habits of the unnatural Western culture. Also, members tend to deal with the social conditions surrounding them in any manner except one which will resolve their disorder. The children of the family unit tend to carry very little priority and immediately tend to become the victims of these negative circumstances, often times used as a scapegoat of strange and unnatural behaviors for any Ancestor to display on the special life form designed to carry them forward eternally. This must be seriously checked and solved immediately, which means that the effects must be eliminated by dealing with the causes.

Family is a commitment in the fullest sense of the word that people make not only to themselves, but to our Creator. Before creating a family structure, one must know and understand enough about their individual selves to be able to identify their personal requirements for compatibility in their quest to serve our Creator and each other. Responsibility covers not only yourself, but it also covers taking care of your family, and your community. Man is in a state of loss, except those who have faith, have good works, and who cooperate with each other for the advancement of true progress for us.

If African-Americans plan on changing their conditions, the changes must be centered around their Ancient Ancestors culture and history, because family exist for the sake of re-creation and reproduction, or it will cease to exist. Family must hold to the same basic morals, principles and values. A family must adhere to the same basic habits and deal with their basic needs in a like manner or it will cease to exist. Also, a family must take the approach that it must exist and it must use any and all available means to ensure that existence. That is, a family must establish itself and it must find a means of achieving harmony and of perpetuating its kind in as large a number as possible. This must be adhered to immediately or both the family structure and the physical, mental and spiritual creations of the family structure and all species involved will eventually disappear.

It is the utmost of importance that we give ourselves a self-examination or reality therapy check- up. We need to analyze our present reality first. The Truth places great emphasis on reality. Life is reality. This is a real world that we live in, and there are real needs that we all must supply for one another. We are cursed, not only because we are Black, we are cursed because we have become a rebellious people toward our Creator and our Ancestors. Going against our nature is suicidal.

A very important clue to why relationships do not

succeed is found in the ignorance of knowing the roles of each participant. Females should look at males for their character and accomplishments, and the males should look at females for their character and cooperation, with love. Support is a fundamental element in considering what a mate can do. As in any other worthwhile activity, one will find his supportive efforts lifted beyond human abilities through the inspired prayer he brings to the situation. His spiritual understanding and steadfast communion with the Creator add a measure of quiet strength to the home atmosphere.

Historically, the Black African man has always been a spiritual being. Spiritual in this sense means an entity that pervades and unifies each area of life. In other words, he believed and practiced a oneness with nature.

Within the framework of ritual and symbolism in which the works of art are seen, the social and political factors must be weighed as a means of showing a general conception of the artist's impression of the universe, it's origin, workings, goal, and meaning in the everyday activities of the people.

Families and communities who have sought to develop naturally in a corrupt environment, without applying revealed knowledge have bought about their own destruction. When man has corrupted his own environment, he must have the guidance of our Creator and our Ancestors, and our Elders (Knowledgeable Ones) in order to establish his life successfully. Therefore, it is important that a religion (a way of life) is used as the base or foundation for life development. If one does not have a healthy relationship with his Creator, how does one expect to successfully function in any environment?

The White world has grown used to seeing the Black world as unthinking, backward and incoherent, so much so that when the African people suddenly appear in a very different light it comes as a shock.

Today, due to slavery and its hypnotic effects of the people of African descent, they now think much like the slave master, who unlike the original man (African) tends to, or better, tries to control nature instead of working with nature or being one with nature. Therefore, for Africans to follow and do something contrary to their nature, or do something innately foreign to them, would be foolish because it would only cause confusion and as a result destruction. When man is faced with difficulty, they must look within themselves, and whether the causes for their troubles are warranted by something that may have been done in our past, which was not in tune with our nature. Perhaps we need to seek the means to rectify the matter: "Be ye in the world, but not of it."

As the Black African historians, Cheikh Anta Diop, Chancellor Williams, Josef ben Jocannon, J. A. Rogers, Dr. Edward Robinson and many other great historians states: "The Black African man has been upon this planet longer than Europeans, and who have built the greatest civilizations all the world has known, practiced a family structure: Polygyny. "

Although Polygyny is unlawful in America; it is more efficient for building a strong nation. Polygyny is an institution whereby a man may marry several wives. This institution can be a solution to people of African descent in America, since the ration of females is much greater than men. J. A. Roger says that at a certain age, the females outnumber the male 42 to 1, which is phenomenal. This is something to seriously consider because it will eliminate competition between women, causing prostitution, loneliness, and being preyed on by other races.

In Ancient societies, and present Eastern societies, without damage to the existing morality, this luxury was and is open to anyone, if he had the means. But, monogamy was the rule at the level of the mass of the people. In so far as Africa, it is considered to be the land of polygyny. It is important to emphasize this fact. In sculpture and pictorial representations, the polygyny of the people is proved by the numerous family structures depicted. Polygyny was general, without ever ceasing to be a sign of social rank. Thus, it is not rare to see members of the lower classes who, seeking to deceive themselves about their own social rank, marry several wives.

The healthy minded person(s) is governed by a strong

moral consciousness. They know innately that there are some things that you just don't do. They know that there are some things that may be left unsaid. The healthy minded person(s) is a listener and a doer, as a result of his or her willingness to follow the process to become or transform into a listener and doer. Beware that the process is not always comfortable. There is always some type of sacrifice, which could be something you are used to having or someone you are accustomed to being with. Remember, "No pain, No gain." Always make it a personal challenge which will cause you to get to know yourself. "Know thy self" applies to the first law of nature.

The socially admitted division of labor reserves to the man, the tasks involving risks, power, force and endurance; if, as a result of a changed situation due to the intervention of some outside factor; cessation of a state of a state of war, and so forth. The woman would carry out the household duties and others reserved to her by society.

It is unthinkable, that an African man share a feminine task with his wife, such as cooking, washing clothes, or rearing children; any European influence, of course, being disregard. The soul's (spirit) requirement on the need in the soul is for enlightenment or intellectual growth. The other need in the soul is for the growth of regard-fulness, proper respect for those things due that regard and respect. Family structure is our salvation!

# People Power

Our frame of reference should come from those before us who looked like us.

If one takes a look at the European influence of the African-Americans in America, you see that there is no structure or specific roles in the family. In fact, you see the man doing female's work, and females doing men's work, and the children doing their own thing. These are the primary signs that the particular family structure or species is on the edge of extinction, and not until a family unit functioning in harmony with nature and the universe is re-established, can any order ever expect to come about to put that family or species back in the evolutionary flow of nature and the universe. From a historical point of view, America was used as a dumping ground for European criminals and other human "refuse." The United States was once called "the graveyard of the white race." England was dumping her convicts, prostitutes, rebels, and discordant elements in America. For a righteous people, by nature, to pattern their lives after a denatured people as this is moving towards extinction.

When the Black African females in America entered the intellectual and industrial field, her sex and her intellect also came into conflict, and it was to be expected that some of them would have as their slogan, "We no longer need men." They were really saying that I don't need a Black man especially when the Black man is not a figure of authority. Females have an assimilative nature which is to become one with authority. Caucasians are almost always looked at as an authority, while the Black man is looked down on, or as less than those in authority.

Naturally, having children is the last thought of this type. The career-minded females have values contrary to her nature, which should be centered around family, and have been altered to adopt the illusionary-destructive values of the Europeans or American females.

This has been a problem with females of African descent since the ideas of the Women's Liberation Movement was created by high-class Jewish women who were tired of staying home cooking and washing the clothes and rearing the children. They can afford to do that because they can hire a family-oriented Black female to take care of their responsibilities, while the homes and families of the Black family is being neglected and destroyed. With this in mind, is there any wonder why there are no Black families, which results with frustration in the Black man, and children going astray. The woman is the determining factor in whether the family will succeed or fail (see the virtuous woman: King James - Holy Bible).

In our culture, the female or mother is the Cultural Scientist. In other words, she passes on, and teaches the children all about where they came from, where they should be (spiritually, mentally, and physically), and where they should be going, Together! She is actually the first teacher and master teacher of her children and all other children. That is called Community (common-unity). Honor thy mother and thy father that your days will be long and prosperous.

Industrialization, with its crowding in cities, and its low wages, compared to the cost of living, is also responsible for production of the mentally and physically defectives, who with the aid of the "destructive" modern medicine and hospitalization, are enabled to propagate their kind, thus inoculating the coming generation, and progressively weakening them. We must also keep in mind the effects of so-called feminism. Under its influence, women are becoming increasingly masculine, especially Black women. In fact, some are female only so far as the primary sexual characters are concerned. So far as the continuance of the race is concerned, the Black woman who never bore a child is, so far as this function is concerned, is a man. Know your purpose!

The Black man is also negligent of his role. He has adopted the European or American "macho" image. In fact, he is so busy trying to develop the physical characters of females, that he is totally against himself. Jerry-curls, polished nails, skin-tight clothes, feminine movements and gestures puts him in an illusionary world of being so-called "hip" and keeping up with the times. What kind of woman in her right mind would want a so-called man of this nature? This type of male is against family because he is so busy trying to be "pretty". Here, we have an eagle hypnotized to believe that he is a chicken or pigeon. Eagles eat them both.

The true Black African leaders in America have always had a hard time trying to teach fools. A fool rejects truth or anyone waking them up to who they really are by nature.

The fool is like the rhinoceros, mentally. The rhinoceros (beast) is near-sighted and whenever he senses anything or anybody of possible danger beyond his range of vision, he charges blindly at it. In the same way, there are those who immediately attack everything that does not happen to fit in with their idea of the true, the beautiful, and the good.

The practice of polygyny is a spiritual function, for the reasons that it is in line with nature. It is no accident that the birth ratio of African males and females is imbalanced. Historically, this family structure was created by Ancient African women. They were intelligent and understanding enough to realize the ratio imbalance, so a group of them, some were sisters, some were cousins, and some were friends that chose one man to manage their affairs; this man was referred to as their husband or head of the family. There was nothing spooky or unnatural about that structure. Keep in mind, the ultimate love the women had for one another to do such a divine thing as that. There was no jealousy, resentment, competition, or manipulation between the family members. The

# *People Power*

Euro-American must have learned a big lesson from this because the foundation of the American Corporations were built from the African family structure of polygyny; which created numbers rapidly, impregnating Black female slaves on the plantation. Breeding was normal.

Ancient Africans believed that nature and God was synonymous. Therefore, for someone to ignorantly say that the birth ratio of Black males to females is an accident, is to say that the Creator has made a mistake. This is highly unlikely, just as it is unlikely for the sun to stop shining all over the world, or for the air we breathe to stop being produced. The high ratio of Black females to Black males, more than any other race, is for the sole purpose of the continuance of their race. Every female is a potential seed nourisher, so if there are more seed nourishers than seed carriers, this race or species should never die. Therefore, we can see that the Black African male and females that decide to practice polygyny are living in accord with nature or the Creator. In fact, this is spiritual understanding. With the foundation starting to take form, a spiritual foundation, in line with nature, we can see that this marriage is not a silly romantic game.

To be spiritually based, we must think right, give right, and eat right, using ancestral culture and heritage as a frame of reference. All ways of life must be culturally centered in order to establish a foundation and to keep it functioning.

The Hon. Haile Baba states that, "An African man's love (selflessness attitude) is to his nation, and an African woman's love (selflessness attitude) is to her mate." With this step properly organized we then can have a "chain of command" in that the male answers to or is obedient to the cultural structure of his nation; the females are to obey the male; and the children are obedient to the females. This is true structure, that will enable the family to have a permanently strong foundation: love-order-balance. With this family structure being executed, the whole family is then obedient to the religion or the Nation. This then will bring about a unity of the church and state, just the way the Creator intended. In fact, the foundation of any society is the family units coming together with one aim, one purpose, and one destiny: Oneness.

True polygyny is a highly structured body of spiritual people, with one head, that teaches about divine principles. The spiritually religious organization teaches correct family structure that will enable all family members to be cared for and protected. The African male must be dedicated and committed to this divine organizational structure with his life; for the level of his dedication will determine the existence of the Nation. In fact, a nation consists of individual family units coming together to build a powerful nation, under righteousness.

After the creation of family, which is the creation of

culture, then institutions must be created to re-enforce or perpetuate culture such as: schools, temples, churches or mosques; politics; jobs; nutrition; hospitals; and etc. Culture must be the center of all institutions. Education, which is essential, is to pass the accumulation of knowledge, wisdom and understanding of a particular people from one generation to the next generation of the like.

It is very important for people of African descent to know what has happened to them to understand their present condition - modern slavery. Knowledge is not going to come to you just because you want knowledge.

Knowledge comes as a result of your faith while you are seeking. "Faith without works is dead:" King James - Holy Bible. Where there is no faith, there is no real knowledge. In the final analysis, people are divided between believers and non-believers.

On the non-believers side you find corrupt people, while on the believers side you find people organized to fight corruption. The female of African Ancestry became the security blanket to ensure the least amount of conflict as it relates to simply black and white. She policed her own children to ensure that they did not get involved in anything non-African or anything opposed to this unnatural order which the Euro-Americans had imposed on them. Her job was to ensure that everyone learned their roles; that European or white children learned that they were superior as "God" had ordained it...and that the children of African Ancestry learned that they were inferior, and born to be slaves and should never think of family or self love or anything other than to work and take care of the master and his children.

The longer the system of slavery existed, the more conditioned she became to the new set of abnormal norms. So much that anytime she detected an African male who rejected this abnormal conditioning, she would report him immediately, even if he was her own son or mate. This would either cause him his life or a serious beating. She had learned to see a proud, self loving man of African Ancestry as a threat to her master's system. Also, she learned to shun and reject those who wanted to live an alternative life if they were to live at all. She learned to admire those who sang and danced to the master's tune. It became a learned fear that the self-loving man would be broken and destroyed by the master, and that the song and dancer would at least be around to keep her warm a few nights as well as breed new slaves as were needed.

As the beautiful Black African-American Queen Sojourner Truth stated, "Slavery was designed to destroy Black males, and it soon sucked the spirit out of Baumfree," who was her father. The African female in America today never learned to have faith in the art of survival, nature and the universe, to the point that it became a sickness to be passed on more severely generation after generation. She took great pride in the master's system and the form of social welfare that she felt a part of and would defend it until her last breath of air.

As a result, the older she became, the more set became her teachings of her mother, who was taught by her mother, who was taught by her mother who had been raped and beaten into submission after watching her sons, brothers, and mate held in chains and beaten to death or into submission by a race of harsh, cruel and very disrespected beasts; having little if any respect for themselves or nature.

These are the same beastly natured creatures who terrorized the entire continent of Africa, by shooting the ancient indigenous Africans and grabbed (stole) their land. These creatures came to Africa with their form of Christianity which is identified as militant and a whole system of oppression: the white man came with a Bible in one hand and a gun in the other. He gave the Black man the Bible while taking his land. He taught the Black man that when master hits the one cheek, you turn the other; and while the white man was enjoying heaven on earth, he wanted the Africans, in America and all over, to believe they would have their share of heaven in the next world (after death).

The churches are a part of the oppressed masses of the country. The white man has raped the Black man's culture and used it as a machine to oppress him. That's why the role of the white missionaries should never be forgiven. The Black man throughout the world is a living symbol of the white man's fear.

Unity promotes balance within each individual who is true to the mission of transforming and renewing their minds toward the beauty of their Ancestors. Faith along with our individual works is necessary. Always know that you are blessed through your efforts, even though some people are blessed through the association with the ones who have already transformed mentally. Always look for the good! Always give one another the benefit of the doubt. We owe that to one another. Be fair to one another!

The struggle for Africans in Americans and all over have been reduced by the white man, by his choice, to black versus white. He has the audacity to talk about the protection of minority groups when he is, in fact, oppressing the majority. In order to destroy the Black Africans, the white man had to destroy their identity from the core of their culture - family. As Sister Winnie Mandela states "If need be, you will use their own methods, because that is the language they understand."

In acknowledging the previous statement, it becomes simpler to understand the present conditions and circumstances of the family structure of African Ancestry in America. The system described has never taken a moment out to rest or to redress itself. It has, rather, evolved through time and processes and has become an indulgence into greater negativity with more by-products. The female of African Ancestry is still forced to assume the role of mother and father, and the older she becomes, the more forceful she becomes in taking on that role.

The male is still following this act. The male of African Ancestry has not taken his role of leader and manager back from the female who is not capable nor designed to fill that role. The male, rather, still allows himself to be used as a stud or service station for females who have become so involved with the exterior system that her concerns with her career take a greater priority than a proper family structure flowing in harmony with their present conditions and circumstances or their off-springs and nature's harmony for them.

Sometimes, especially in times of difficulty, we as parents have a tendency to compromise firmness because of the fear of losing our childrens' respect or love. We must not let needed "tough love" become soft, or we will lose both the respect and love of our children. Maybe because of that, we may even lose them spiritually. The boundaries must be kept intact. For peace and strength, the family must remain even more firmly based in the tradition of our Ancestors.

The responsibility for the socialization and education lies with the family. African-Americans must stop expecting government, integration, remediation and the like to do for their children what they should do themselves.

Who knows more about socializing and educating your children than you, Black people?! If the children are to be "saved" in the full sense of that word, then there must come about a complete cultural revolution in the Black community. New values, standards, attitudes, etc., must become common in the community. Socialize and educate your children for mastery and control, to be the best among all people and not a servant to any people.

Each person must be the one who takes responsibility for properly socializing their child or children. You must provide him or her with the materials and opportunities which will aid positive growth toward full manhood or womanhood and mastery. It will not cost much money, only time, and sincere consistent effort.

It is very important that one understands how conditions and environment are conducive to the physical, mental, and spiritual formation, or deformation of the character of a person or a people. The environment dictates one's behavior and outlook on life. Beware of the city life, which produces an unnatural way of thinking, giving and eating. City life is hard life-concrete and asphalt which is unnatural for us as a people. We need open land.

We are gregarious people by nature. Group oriented people by nature! Someone planted weeds in our gardens (minds) while we were not paying attention. We are always surrounded by negative forces in this world, so put your armor on (Focus) and keep them on. We did not become what we are today by accident. Our confusion and wickedness came from those who we were controlled by. So stop blaming yourself and each other for the things that we were made into by being forced to be the way that we have become by being taught to be against yourself, and all others that look like you. In other words, we have been brainwashed to hate ourselves by design. Redemption is a practice that is necessary to recover. We must do all we can to recover, by Healing ourselves for the Team, which is each other. Get yourself together for the Team that you belong to first. Remember, the first Law of Nature is Self Preservation, for the Team that looks like you. No individual is more important than the Team because the Team is only as strong as the weakest one. So, let us lift up each other to the level of Divineness! Together We Will Stand and Divided We Will Fall. Choose you this day says the Lord. Where there is a will, there is a way. Believe that, because some of us have found a way, which means that some of us have been Blessed with some answers. Beware that in the world, the good (God) ones are hated with no just cause. In spite of it all, do all that you can to make a contribution to your recovery and your people (Team). Everyone have to earn their blessings. So Be Blessed My People! Avoid the road to destruction-hell. Continue to earn your rights to be chosen by the Most High and your team players (your family, your people). We Can Do It and We Will No Doubt Win!

## NOTES

## NOTES

# Chapter IV

# Economics

One of the greatest attitudes to take towards being successful is that of being willing to try a new way, a new approach, or a new method, rather than continuing to lament your present difficulties. Each person has been endowed with the ability to make a choice. Every choice should be a learning situation to move your knowledge and understanding to a higher consciousness.

Each individual is defined by their choices they make. Remember all choices have a future. When you know and see a consistent pattern of one's behavior, then you must acknowledge that. In other words, ask yourself, "How many times does a person have to show me who they are before I start believing them?" Some people we give a free pass to say and do what they want, and they will be the ones who hurt us the most, especially the more you care for them. If it is what it is, then it is what it is. If you don't face their reality, they can cause permanent damage. The more you care, the more damage can be cause, because all damage is not repairable. That is why a lot of people hurt so bad because they can not seem to get over certain experiences. A lot of courage and willpower will definitely get you through. All damage is not repairable! Fight hard and smart to regain your balance because you owe that to yourself. Don't Let Yourself Down, No matter What!!! Keep in mind that hurt people hurt people. If you love and respect yourself, then you will always be in a preventive mindset. You owe that to yourself, Family. "Be ye in the world but not of it." That requires that you continue to transform and renew your mind intentionally. You are always blessed through your efforts. No efforts, no blessings. A lot of efforts, a lot of blessings. We must get over people's titles because if you don't, they can cause you to destroy yourself permanently just because you care so much for them. Do not volunteer to be a fool for a fool, because it can cause you to lose your life forever. All attitudes and choices should be centered around culture. Keep in mind that culture is a generator of economics. Cultural concepts create economic value. Also keep in mind that all choices have a future. In other words, be careful what or who you choose because it will be there tomorrow with its effects, circumstances, or results. Never go head long into any situation without first checking it out with clear thought. Don't be deceived by saying and believing that you do your best work under pressure. Your best work is done when you have a clear and peaceful mind.

## *People Power*

Take a deep breathe before you approach a situation. You will be thankful that you did.

The economic problem with African-Americans is that they need to create an economic value system centered around ancestral cultural. First, they must recognize and admit that they are Africans born in America. All ethnic groups have nationalistic roots, whereby they can identify themselves to a particular geographic area, culture, language, race, tradition, religion, and history. Due to racism in America, or people of African Ancestry have been stripped of everything that gives them identity from an original historical point of view. As a result, they identify with someone else culture which is contrary to their nature.

As long as we continue to be economic slaves to our ways, created by our negative attitudes and ignorance, we will continue to create the results that are happening today in our communities. As a result of this we continue to create the following: ignorance of self; disrespect for one another; police brutality; DHS stealing or kidnapping our children; welfare buying the souls of our women; women selling the souls of our children; and depending on the government that does not care for us. The bottom line is that we must wake up and stop pretending that it is not that bad and ask ourselves how good is it?!

Racism is above all factors and variables the most detrimental factor that has been at work against African-

Americans in the past 400 years or more influencing our ability to survive or cease to exist. When people are about survival, or are desperate, they do little or no thinking. They mostly react on how they feel, which is one of the problems or mistakes that African-Americans make. Never decide when you are not at peace with yourself.

Emotions can and will cloud your ability to think clearly. In fact, racism is continuous and unyielding. Europeans have adopted the attitude that they are better and more intelligent than any non-European, especially the people of African Ancestry.

Beware that economics in America was created specifically to make you buy products that you don't need or buy products that do not produce the results that they should. This is what you call deception. It causes you to feel you are getting one thing, when all along, you are getting something else: Economic Illusions.

The only thing that can move a power is a greater power. Why do Europeans oppress Africans and other people of color? Is it because they fear the God given power in these people? Historically, Africans are said by many to be the most powerful people physically, mentally, and above all spiritually. The word Africa means the land of the "gods" or "spirit" people. Also, historically the Berlin Conference was held especially to divide the most sort after and richest geographical area on earth, by the Europeans, which was the continent of Africa or

Alkebulan (original name). This continent is still today occupied by Europeans and Arabs, one way or another.

Africans must realize that they have the same enemies and problems before they can begin the struggle to unite. They have been fighting effects and illusions for centuries and they are in worst condition than ever before. If the causes are not dealt with, the same effects and illusions will exist. The main cause is that they need to know who they are, which will motivate a change. Most Blacks in America will not admit that they are people of African Ancestry, and that creates the ability only to survive and eventually perish. There has been a total change or decline in culture. Usually, this is most often seen when the life of a people is suddenly and violently altered by forced migration into an unfavorable environment, by destructive wars, plagues, famines, and other calamities, or by mixture with an inferior people.

The conditions that hold African-Americans in poverty are both internal and external. Internal are those factors that you have substantial control such as: education, energy, creativity, contacts, job skills, choice of mate, emotions, actions, knowledge, and so forth.

Among the external factors are those that you cannot control such as: weather, peoples' thoughts, interest rates, and racism. As mentioned before, racism is the most detrimental factor of keeping a people in bondage, which produces degradation and dehumanization.

This is a sickness and very unnatural in the eyesight of the Creator. All nations that have practiced racism throughout history have had a sudden and violent fall. Were we better off being segregated?

A solution to overcoming racism is to become serious about yourself, your people (race), and your goals, say what you mean and mean what you say, and force the opposing parties to respect you and what you stand for, then you will find certain racists (white folks or others) ready to do business. Even though they may be racist, most of them are not crazy, especially when it comes to the pocket book. "The love of money is the root of all evil": Holy Bible - King James.

African-Americans must examine everything, eliminate all signs of waste and direct our energies to the major task of building an economic base. It must have structure which should be centered around their culture and heritage. Elimination just does not only imply taking something from you, but gives something to you. If you can discipline yourself so that you don't allow outside influences to take you to the things that you know will bring you down, then you will be successful in your life affairs. If you do not discipline yourself in that way, then you are sure to be a failure and a coward, because you won't even challenge yourself. Self check-ups should be a regular thing to do for yourself. How would you know or get to know yourself if you avoid doing that for yourself. The First Law of Nature is to Know Thyself. For if you know who you are, then you will know who God is. Self Awareness is more powerful than anything else.

The saying that "money is the root of all evil" must have been created by some rich person or persons. If you look at the purpose of money, how can it be evil unless an evil minded person(s) is handling it. Europeans would have others believe that the most important thing you should think about everyday would be how to do your job better. Making money would be looked at as some kind of sick, selfish, social disease.

If you look at the attitudes of capitalist, you find that this is true, which is the social structure of America. Capitalist are greedy and vicious evil minded people who would do anything for the love of money and power.

All prophets and messengers of God taught their people how to avoid wicked and evil people. These people of God were vessels or catalyst that were used to bring a people out of bondage. If people only listen and imitate God's vessels, they could rise above oppression. Their message was always, to come from among those evil people and put your God first, to enter the kingdom of heaven. We must remember that God gave us the earth to have dominion over and build your heaven. But, the oppressor taught that you have to die physically to go to heaven, which are the teachings of Christianity (white nationalism) to the so-called slaves: Africans.

White people should live by the philosophy that because a person is born of a different color doesn't mean that he is your enemy.

We must begin today to control the flow of currency (money) in our communities. Economic empowerment and moral strength is the winning combination that we need in order to have a happy new life. One without the other will be short lived. Our morals resemble our communities. We have been trained and duped into a stupor to disrespect ourselves and each other and move quickly towards self-destruction. We have to do all that we can to develop and maintain healthy and respectful relationships towards each other: Community.

For a little over 6,000 years, historically speaking, the Caucasian has been making war with people all over the world. There have been wars between Whites and Africans, Whites and Asians, Whites and Indians, Whites and Orientals, Whites and Whites, etc. Looking at this serious and important point, one can truly see who the racist are. Also, anyone who adopts the philosophies of these racist are in fact racist themselves.

Everywhere these racist put their feet, you can almost guarantee trouble. These deceitful and evil beasts come into your country as a friend and they end up with your land and everything on it, including you. Missionaries were the soldiers of Satan for the specific purpose to cause confusion between the indigenous people in order to divide and conquer, and to steal your land using any means necessary.

These so-called Christians still exist today and Africa being the main target is continuously catching more hell then anyone can imagine.

Unification, using the principles of the prophets and messengers of God, is the only solution. These are some of the examples: Moses, Noah, Abraham, Jesus, John the Baptist, Muhammad, Elijah Muhammad, Nkrumah, Marcus Garvey, Malcolm X, and Dr. Haile Baba. Their cry was to put God first, by loving one another and to do for self. Even though all Blacks are of African Ancestry, who are of different religious tribes, they are in reality a part of the One. You can not enslave a people if God is first in their lives. The big problem with people who have been enslaved is that they have left their God-Principles. In order to know God, one must first "Know Thyself" for God is within.

The enslavement took from African-Americans the dignity of unity: family. They knew that the strength of a people is in the unity of their family. Therefore, to accomplish their goals, they had to destroy the foundation which is the family bond. Today, the lack of family unity is at the root of our many societal problems. If one accepts the guidance of our Creator and Ancestors, we can re-establish our family unity and bring dignity back to family life and thus to be a society that is compatible to their nature.

People of African Ancestry have been around evil and wickedness so long that they have adopted the beliefs and lifestyles of them. Man's mission for success must be greater than himself. If there is something in you that is not of righteousness, then you must remove it. You have to be as a cemented structure by coming together as one with righteousness as the foundation. Ancestry is the frame of reference.

If you look at history, in 1555, John Hopkins bought Africans to Jamestown, Virginia as slaves, but the official date was 1619. The reason for this is because it took the white man 64 years to break the spirits of The Africans in order to enslave them mentally. Most African-Americans today still have those evil attributes in them that were forced in them. They must know the causes to eliminate the effects. As a result, they have in fact become their own worst enemy.

Since slavery was forced labor, we adopted the attitude that "I hate work" or "I'll work enough to survive" because work did not improve the life of the laborer, his family or his community; instead, it improved the life, family and community of the slave master.

In the Ancient African societies and other natural societies, work is looked upon with pride. During slavery, work was used as a punishment. Since work was used as a punishment, the slaves despised it. If you take a serious look at African-Americans, even today, they refer to work as slavery; consequently, equating freedom with the avoidance of work. For instance, look at the boys on the corner wasting time, playing sports on the playgrounds, or watching T.V., who feels that "I am not going to be nobody's slave" or "I am not going to have no one bossing me around and telling me what to do." Today, work is something that is approached unwillingly and generally out of necessity.

As a result of the above, African-Americans have developed bad habits to avoid work, such as stealing, gambling, hustling people, and/or get-rich-quick schemes. All of this is because of the adopted attitude of our hatred of work. Is there any wonder why we don't have any businesses we can call our own. If we work, we would rather work for someone else simply because there is a periodic salary and a work schedule. This creates an illusion of leisure, among others. The society has, in fact, developed such a leisure orientation that work has come to be something to be despised, not only by Africans, but by all members of the society. Man is free, or should be free, in the sense that his actions are self-determination- Kujichagulia, that they flow from his natural nature. Self-development is the worth inculcated in human beings. It means the full unfolding of the self on the actualization of all it's potentialities. Amen-Ra!!!

Most people look at a job as an end in itself rather

than a means to greater ends. America has so much status, value and self-concept is tied to what a person does for a living, many people would rather collect welfare or unemployment than work on a job, which they believe belittles them. This is a result of the job's low pay and prestige.

African-Americans must learn the art of selling, manufacturing; and enjoy it because America is a big market where everything is for sale.

Even though Black folks will never get their fair share of jobs in this country, we need to create jobs for ourselves. Since racism is at a height, the only way to combat it is to unite and become independent in businesses. Why work for a racist all of your life when you can work for your damn self and create an economic empire of your own which will create jobs for other Blacks? If you are going to work for whites then work long enough to create enough money to start a business that you can call your own. God bless the child who got his own mind and works hard and starts to have his own everything.

The Seven Principles of Kwanzaa-Nguzu Saba by Dr. Molana Ron Karenga include the following:

<u>Umoja</u> (Unity): To strive for and to maintain unity in the family, community, nation, and race.

<u>Kujichagulia</u> (Self-Determination): To define ourselves, name ourselves, create for ourselves, and speak for ourselves.

Ujima Collective Work and Responsibility): To build and maintain our community together and make our brothers' and sisters' problems our problems, and to solve them together.

Ujamaa (Cooperative Economics): To build and maintain our own stores, shops, and other businesses and to profit from them together.

Nia (Purpose): To make our collective vocation the building and developing of our community in order to restore our people to their traditional greatness.

Kuumba (Creativity): To do always as much as we can, in the way we can, in order to leave our community more beautiful and beneficial than we inherited it.

Imani (Faith): To believe with all our hearts in our people, our parents, our teachers, our leaders, and the righteousness and victory of our struggle.

Independence comes in stages like everything else, but you must stand and start somewhere. A lot of successful people started with a produce stand, a hot dog stand, a clothing stand, etc., and created enough money to open their own store front. Don't be too prideful to start at a small level, as long as you keep your goals in front of you.

Purpose is always the determining factor to be successful in all areas of Life. Everybody has to crawl before they walk. A system and discipline are the two things that makes money. Black businesses should be solely owned by Black people, located in the community, and patronized by Blacks. We must learn how to keep our money mainly circulating in our communities. Businesses should be created according to the needs of the people which will determine the growth and longevity of the business.

The business owner must keep in mind that most people don't buy what they need or do what they need to do. People mostly deal with their wants. They want what they want! Get It!?

You may come along as a good guy and try to give the people what you think they need, maybe even what they think they need, but they will still want what they want. I once opened a health food store in the Black community, but it did not succeed as it should because people wanted the usual death dealing foods. Anything that is not popular will not last long in business unless the white man put his stamp of approval on it. I recalled that most of my health food products sold after the white radio and T.V. stations approved it. Most of the times they will go out of their way to go to a white store. This has to discontinue because the white businesses do not benefit the Black communities at all. In fact, all of the money is taken out of the Black communities to develop the white communities. If you don't believe me, check it out for yourself. That even applies to all foreigners who set up shop in our communities. They take All of the money to their communities, and prosper very well. African-Americans need to establish a set of rules that if others set up shop in our communities that they have to contribute to the upliftment of that particular community. That is only fair if the foreigners really care. If they don't comply, then Do Not go in their stores, which means that they will eventually close. It's all about Respect!

Over 200 billion dollars a year is spent by Blacks in America and it is in vain because the only ones who are not benefiting are Blacks. Why? Because it is spent everywhere but in their communities. If it is spent in the community, most of the times, the businesses are owned by non-Blacks; that is a major problem. You can't blame no one for poor communities except for the people who are living in them, because they set the standards which determines the economic level and the conditions of the community.

Non-Blacks analyze Black communities to see what they like and then they open a business and sell what they (Blacks) like. They also find out that Blacks usually buy what they want, rather than what they need as a family unit, so non-Blacks go into business to provide Blacks with their wants. Keep in mind that the only reason that non-Black businesses exists in the Black communities is because Blacks patronize them and then feel a false sense of security of getting something better, than if it was a Black owned business. This is an attitude that has been passed down from slavery. But this attitude must be changed so that the business owners and the communities can change for the benefit of the people who live there.

Money is one of those forbidden topics that people don't like to talk too much about. The most people do is complain about money or the lack of it.

In America, you cannot do much of anything without money because money almost means everything; besides sex and games, which is also a high priority in America. Most people are ignorant of making money for the purpose of building a financial base. We should learn what wealth is and how to measure it, which means that we should have access to large amounts of money. It can be savings accounts, your home, stocks and bonds, gold, jewelry and many other ways. Money creates options!

We should understand that our own habits keep us in the poor house. For instance, we spent 15 million dollars a year on chewing gum. We are chewing our lives away! Also, Black people spend more money on non-essentials than any other people, which creates a major problem: foolish spending and buying will put anyone in the poor house sooner or later. Because we are at the bottom of the economic scale, it will do us a lot of good to spend or buy only for necessities with the purpose of creating a financial base to start your own business or investment.

## People Power

We have very little understanding of the strong influence that our own attitudes have about ourselves, money, work, life, and time in general effect our ability to gain and build economics. We must respect money for its purpose.

It is easy to blame America as the cause of our poverty, but it is our fault to stay that way. We should learn our history and understand that we are by nature gregarious people. Associating, sharing, loving, caring, respecting, being sensitive, compassionate, etc. are the natural acts towards one another by our ancestors. The reason why we are in a worst condition today than ever is because we are getting farther away from our natural existence. Individualism and other adopted attitudes are destroying us. The only way to prevent total destruction is to learn our history, culture, religion, language and tradition, for without this we will remain naked and defenseless before the entire world. All of our godly messengers and prophets have warned us for literally hundreds of years, but we continue to turn a deaf ear and live in total ignorance, and we wonder why we continue to be used and abused by anyone and everyone. It is written on the walls to "Know Thyself" which brings about knowledge, wisdom and understanding of self and others. We must become aware that America exists on our ignorance and our attacks on each other.

The truth will and can show you where you have

failed and where you need to get to. Always embrace your history and traditions because it gives you purpose and direction. We must stop living and walking in the dark pretending that it is not that bad. Then ask yourself, how good is it? If I know who I am, then I know who God is. God is always within. So, tap into the power within! You will always be successful.

We need to understand the things that we profess to know. For instance, what good is the teachings of God's messengers and prophets if we don't apply the principles towards today's situations? The teachings must be applied on time without altering the truth. All of us need to be in an intense period of study because we need to know to the level of understanding. Our opinions and beliefs and theories have not gotten us anywhere, we need a major overhaul. Principle must be the basis in our lives, which is the substance of God. When you take things for granted, you do things that you think or feel is right which often times you are wrong and things are in a hell of a condition. A word to the wise, know our-story and not so much just his-story (non-Africans). Every person of African Ancestry are gods and goddess by nature, but most have become fools by circumstances.

If we don't improve the quality of our lives we will self destruct. Ask yourself, "What am I doing today to improve myself for the benefit of my people?" We must get in the field of study and work. We must help self as a pre-requisite of helping others. We are so busy looking at each other negatively, that we fail to look at the real cause, which is oneself. We have to clean up ourselves. The most important thing is to get into self. Each person has the ability to shape and fashion himself or herself (character) according to their thoughts. Keep in mind that white folks used knowledge to suppress us into slavery because of our ignorance of ourselves and who the wicked white man is. "Study to show thyself approved unto God, a workman that needeth not to be ashamed, rightly dividing the word of truth." (King James Holy Bible; 2nd Timothy 2:15). Seek and ye shall find. Be careful of what you are seeking. Remember Cause and Effect! We spend more money and time killing ourselves, and allowing others to kill us, then we spend to live and stay healthy as a people. We need to attain the desire to get knowledge and understanding, from the the cradle, to the grave.

This will free us from the chains of racism. This must not be prolonged, it must be immediately acted upon. We must do for self and be independent of other people. We must put our money back into our communities. The majority of us, including our so-called leaders, have been brain washed and conditioned to believe things that are contrary to our natural existence. We must expose ourselves as much as possible to our-story. We must learn the disciplines: science, music, art, etc. to give us a foundation. We need to wake up from our hypnotic and programmed state and realize the beauty in ourselves through our history and culture. All of our work is doing for others. When are we going to do for ourselves and build an economic base?

Our main purpose for existing is to do the will of the Creator. The way we must do this is by building character in line with principle: God. Study and work to show yourself approved unto God. This is the duty of each individual person of African Ancestry. Let us continue to respect and honor our people by representing them at all times. We must finally consider developing the concept of Sankofa, which means we have to go back and embrace, to bring forth, those things that worked for us in the pass. Always remember where you come from because you might have to go back and get, and validate it. Put aside your pride and get busy Spiritually.

## NOTES

## NOTES

# Chapter V

# Conclusion

Unfortunately, most African-Americans are made to be robot thinkers. This is to say that they don't think at all. When faced with a problem, they do practically everything but get right down with the cause of solving them by reflection and logical thinking. They have a tendency to rely on the so-called authorities or whatever they have been told in response to their questions.

There is a great need for balance. What I mean by balance is to have good judgment and mental stability. There must be balance in everyone's life, to study, to love, to respect, to help one another, and to unite. In essence, it means growth towards a righteous way of life.

Ignorance and misconceptions predominate in the lifestyles and thoughts of most African-Americans which has been passed down through the ages from slavery. This is unfortunate for attaining a healthy and successful way of life. Our biggest task is in deprogramming ourselves of all the misconceptions that have been imbedded in your intellectual cosmogony. Then we will be able to understand and act upon the messages of our true leaders and what our great ancestors taught from the Motherland - Alkebulan (one of the original name).

We have not really tapped into our powers that are

within each one of us. I can truly say that we are in very much need of the Almighty Creator (God). It is time for us to put away childish things and become a Man (mind). Our Father (God) loves His own. He does not love everybody as was taught to the so-called Negroes in America. He only loves those who are striving, sincerely to do righteous deeds. One can safely say that He hates the wicked, and has a burning fire (hell) for them that will not repent.

A nationalistic way of thought is our only solution, but everything must start from within each individual. A misconception of nationalism is that those who believe in it are racist. The true nationalist is never a racist because he or she strives to bring about a cohesive spirit among his people. Once it is accepted, the movement becomes widely adaptable by those to whom it came. The message from a nationalist is always aimed at his people for the benefit of all. Those who accept the teachings of nationalism must adhere to the behavior, lifestyles, customs, cultural habits, and whatever else that is accepted by those particular people to whom the words were first given.

We must become team players. In other words, get your individual self together for the team (the group). Therefore, if anyone outside of the team harm you, they have to deal with the team. Unity is the key to longevity. In order for a team to be successful, there must be complete cooperation from each individual. Everyone must be All-In!

Man is created with aims and purpose and we as individuals must seek to find what they are, which would be for the benefit of something bigger than yourself. Knowledge should be put into practice towards Nationhood. We must understand that principle means Unity. The principles of life must be taught by the ones who are blessed with the knowledge and understanding. The more we bring out our true nature, the more we bring out the God in us. For we are the very expression of God. We are an under-developed people because of our lack of understanding, and understanding comes by way of continuously hearing the truth.

We must not forget what has happened to us for the past 400 years, because within those years you will find the causes of our present conditions. The only way that one can change his circumstances is to find the cause and realize that there must be a change in the cause. If we reject what we have learned and reprogram ourselves to the truth, then and only then can our condition change to benefit us. There must be a change and it must start from within. Law of Karma!

The most difficult task people have in their lives is keeping their thoughts in line with nature. For we can never arrive at a harmonious adjustment to life or to people, until we learn to get along with ourselves. Most people struggle all their lives with this "self" they live with, without coming to some terms, to understand themselves, to make some attempt to get along. We must develop the courage to "turn the page".

You cannot get away from yourself. In yourself is your heaven and your hell. In yourself is everything you will ever need. However, you cannot tap into this great power until you learn to manage your mind or thoughts, your thoughts are seeds that grow into reality. If you have a feeling of love for another, it is because you have planted the thought of love in yourself first. If you are resistant toward another brother or sister, it is because you have some kind of conflict within yourself.

When you are overly critical of your brother or sister, it is because you feel inferior to them. When you are understanding of others, it is because you feel secure within yourself. Your attitudes toward yourself influence everything you do, everything you think, and every relationship you have. Everything starts from within and proceeds outward.

Therefore, we can see that African-Americans due to slavery, have a very bad picture of themselves. This bad or negative image produces bad and negative results in their lives. We can now see that it is very important that we learn to manage our thoughts and emotions; but which thoughts and feelings are the ones that most affect our lives, you may ask? The thoughts and feelings that you first have about yourself. Everything starts with self!

A great example of a person using a positive mental management technique is Muhammad Ali. This brother convinced himself that he is "The Greatest" therefore, others saw him the same way he saw himself. Your state of mind should always be conditioned to think that you are potentially the greatest person at whatever you decide to do in the world. Potentiality is the great key, the great truth. Potentially you are the best, the greatest, for potentially you are the perfect God-idea. You are the direct descendant of the Ancient Africans who built the greatest civilizations the world has ever known, be it yesterday or today. There is no one quite like you! We need to keep our thoughts stayed on our responsibilities, rather than on our weaknesses. Your weaknesses conceal your strengths.

Self-knowledge is another key to master positive, mental management. The more we know ourselves, the more we unmask the many layers of illusions and stereotypes, that make up our external nature. Eventually, we will come to know that within ourselves is the potential of that which we were created to be: Godly! Always work towards your Godhood!

Recognize that we are not Europeans, but rather of African Ancestry, and that in order to harmonize with our present circumstances and conditions, we must seek specific solutions that relate specifically with our own unique ancestry. We must also recognize that presently, due to many negative circumstances that were put upon us by others and ourselves, there is a shortage of males of African Ancestry, but a great demand. We must recognize that nature and universal law provides a positive solution for that problem.

It is greed, selfishness and utter stupidity, which has been bred into the male and female of African Ancestry that interferes with nature's natural solution. Therefore, it causes more conflict and negativity which aids in the destruction of the original people. We must realize that the reason why people of African Ancestry kill each other is because they were trained to kill one another, as a result of self-hate which was taught by the slave master. Everything you do is in accord with your conscious level.

We must set our own goals and use time to our advantage to achieve our goals. There is nothing new about planning your way to success. Our African Ancestors at all times have dared to do so. Over and over, in the face of insurmountable obstacles, they have succeeded while others without a plan have failed. What they planned for, they achieved. You can plan for success and achieve it too!

By writing down your desires, you are getting definite in planning your success, and you make contact with the friendly visible and invisible forces all about you that wish to help your dreams come true. Your written and spoken words move on the spiritual ether, above time, space, and circumstances, to produce successful results for you.

The reason why you can plan your way to success is this: When you list your desires, make a success covenant, or work out a master plan for success, you are basically doing one important thing; you are choosing what you want instead of worrying about that which you do not want. The word "choose" is a magic word to the mind. Our Creator gives us the birth right to choose. Choose you this day says the Lord of all. What you see is what you get. Also remember, it is nothing until you call it. So, be careful what you call it because it is only real to you. Our Father gives each person the ability to choose and call it what you may. Always look for the good (God). For God Is Good, Forever!!!

Your mind constantly works through what you choose. When you choose what you want, you feed your mind with the mental equivalent of whatever it is you have chosen, and your mind gets busy trying to produce your choice as a result. In other words, the conscious mind gives the subconscious mind the authority to produce the results. So, be careful what you ask for or desire. Thoughts are seeds that will grow. Every time you think a particular thought, it produces the results accordingly. Be careful what you think of. Thoughts Are Things! Where much is given, much is required!

All things are done by choice. This is our African Ancestor's mystery school teachings.

When you make a choice, you open the way to results. Experience will convince you that your practice of choosing produces results. Things always happen after decisions are made. Make a mental habit of deliberate, bold, direct choosing of what you want. This causes a decision to be made in your thinking, and results always follow a strong decision. Your mental choice produces results, but it is up to you to make that mental choice first. Regardless what your present circumstances or conditions are, you can change them by first making a choice, creating a plan, and then act on the plan. Always practice patience!

The serious minded builder must sacrifice. He or she must plan for the future and must understand that the real value of their work (mental and physical) will only really be obvious at a later time. In other words, there must be delayed gratification. Patience is the key! Can you keep on moving constructively while the "storm" is going on? You will be tested and tried. No one is exempt! Never be afraid of a challenge that will move you forward divinely. Everything Is In Divine Order. So, keep the connection to Divine Order and then you will experience many blessings that life has to offer. God does not make mistakes, but we do. But, if you learn from your mistakes, then it is all good. "Seek And Ye Shall Find", "Knock And The Door Will Be Opened." Do you believe that?

If our actions are in accord with the time, our actions will definitely bare positive and beneficial results. Freedom implies responsibility. We all have to be responsible for what happens to ourselves, as well as our communities and what takes place in them. Harambee!

*People Power*

## NOTES

## NOTES

# AUTHOR'S BIOGRAPHY

Dr. Sadiki Che' Baye is an educator, entrepreneur, author, counselor in relationships and life skills, and is a very spiritual man. He has earned many degrees from major institutions: Chowan College: Associate of Science Degree; Temple University: Bachelor of Science in Education; Pan African Federation Organization (PAFO): Bachelor of Historical Education; Institute of Ancient African Religious Science: Bachelor of African Life Studies; Temple University: Master of Education and Certificate of Education Administration; Victory Institute: Doctor of Religious Counseling and; Alkebulan Institute: Minister of Education. He has also served as an instructor in the Philadelphia public schools and for PASCEP in the Pan African Studies Department at Temple University, and recently initiated into the Buffalo Soldiers as Captain.

Even though this is his first major book publication, it is very truthful and has an abundant amount of wisdom. Please enjoy the words of truth and get motivated to make a bigger difference for those who are in dire need of you and each other. As long as you are growing (spiritually, mentally and physically), you cannot go wrong. Keep on climbing to higher grounds of life. Enjoy the journey of this truthfully put book which have many "pearls of wisdom" in it. There is more to come!!!

# BE PURPOSEFUL !!!

Our main purpose as individuals is to get ourselves together for the team - your people. No man is made to be alone. It took a team to get you here (your father and mother), and it will take a team to sustain you. Life is about the survival of the fittest! Prepare to take your rightful position to contribute and uplift the team's purpose.

Total cooperation is necessary! Each one has to give others a reason to be there for them as a team member. Let us all be excellent in our efforts to be the best that we can! Everyone is truly blessed through your efforts. To be the best, you have to do your best. It is all about the process! You can't win football using baseball rules, even though both are ball games. Be very clear about your purpose, which is determined by fulfilling the process that is compatible to your existence!

Harambe'!!!

(Let Us All Pull Together)

# COMMENTARY

*"For more than 35 years, Dr. Sadiki Che' Baye has been a consultant and mentor to the Bridgeway Community, Inc. and to those who needed his understanding, experience and support throughout the Philadelphia area."*

- Emily Hill Rollins, Executive Director and Servant To The Community

*"Dr. Sadiki Che' Baye has superb critical thinking skills to produce a thought provoking body of work that has an excellent correlation of ancient African culture and the current issues that affect African-Americans."*

- Sister Sandra (Abanaa) Carter, M. Ed.

*"Dr. Sadiki Che' Baye has written this astoundingly, intellectually, prominently, thought provoking, high standard, executive agenda, expertise in the field, book of cultures, rights, regulations, of our beautiful culture, our journey from and to a diverse society. In which, in this book, Dr. Sadiki explains every course of this great divide, on how to pay attention to these dedicated truths, adhering to them and once read, you will never forget. In doing so you would have arrived years earlier with much integrity. This book is more than a beginning, its forward rules of life is a royal teaching of an intellectual beautiful people that God has ordained to live and let live!"*

- Florence Rosie Givens, Author Poet

# BIBLIOGRAPHY

Dr. Haile Baba Olugbala Amen-Ra: Alkebulan Maga-zine, Alkebulan Press, (1980)

J. A. Rogers: Africa's Gift to America, Published (1959); Revised and Expanded , (1989): Helga Rogers

Chiekh Anta Diop: Black Africa: The Economic and Cultural Basis for a Federated State; Chicago, Review Press, (June 1, 1987); The Cultural Unity of Black Africa

Josef ben Jocahannan: Africa: Mother of Western Civilization, Black Classic Press, (1988)

Chancellar Williams: The Destruction of Black Civilization, Third World Press, (February 1, 1992)

Pan Africa Federation Organization (PAFO): The Journey of the Songhai People, Dr. Edward W. Robinson, Jr., Calvin R. Robinson, Redman Battle, Farmer Press, (January 1, 1987)

King James Version: The Holy Bible, Harper Collins, (2001)

Marcus Mosiah Garvey: Marcus Garvey Chronicles,The Back To Africa Movement, Afchron, Com., (March 5, 2005)

Malcolm X: Malcolm X Speaks, Edited With Prefatory Notes By George Breitman, Grove Press, New York, (1965)

Amos N. Wilson: The Developmental Psychology of The Black Child, Africana Research Publications, New York, (1978)

Mark Hyman: Blacks Before America I, II, III, Bell of Pennsylvania, (1978)

Dr. Frances Cress Welsing: The Isis Papers: The Keys to The Colors, Third World Press, (December 1, 1991)

Maulana Ron Karenga: Kwanzaa "A Celebration of Family, Community and Culture, African-American Cultural Center, Los Angeles, CA, (1966)

Carter G. Woodson: The Mis-Education of the Negro, Start Publishing LLC, (2012)

Marcus Tullius Cicero: Tusculan Disputation, Digireads. Com, (2007)

Dr. Silvano Senn: Sonoma Whole Health Dentist, University of California (San Francisco), (2005)

Shahrazad Ali: How Not To Eat Pork, Or Life Without Pork, Civilized Publications, (June 1, 1985)

Sojourner Truth: Narrative of Sojourner Truth (An African-American Heritage Book), Wilder Publications, (August 1, 2008)

Winnie Madikizela-Mandela: Long Walk To Freedom, The Guardian, (January 5, 2014)

www.ingramcontent.com/pod-product-compliance
Lightning Source LLC
Chambersburg PA
CBHW072254270326
41930CB00010B/2378